medicare 1

Starting your Medicare Journey

case publications

table of contents

book description

dispel the cloud of uncertainty surrounding medicare!

Are you or a loved one approaching retirement age and finding yourselves lost in the labyrinth that is Medicare?

Are you terrified of overlooking crucial details or making costly mistakes?

Perhaps you're already inundated with generic online guides, government publications, advice from family and friends, and materials from insurance companies - each claiming to be the ultimate guide yet leaving you more confused than ever.

You're not alone. In fact, Medicare is one of the most challenging topics for seniors. The complexity of rules and the risk of making costly mistakes can cause unnecessary stress, precisely when you need to focus on enjoying retirement.

But here's the good news: There's finally a comprehensive guide to help you make sense of Medicare!

Introducing the definitive book that bridges the gaps, clarifies confusing jargon, and most importantly, imparts practical, actionable advice for navigating the Medicare maze.

This guide takes you by the hand and leads you through the intricacies of Medicare so you make a well-informed decision that optimizes your coverage while minimizing costs.

Here's a peek at what you'll find within this insightful guide:

- **Demystify the Medicare Enrollment** - Understand when and how to enroll, with a keen focus on avoiding late enrollment penalties.
- **"Do I Need to Enroll at 65?"** - Explore this question in-depth, answering all the doubts you never knew you had.
- **Practicality** - Practical checklists, cheat sheets, and templates to help you organize and plan for your future.
- **Enlightening Comparisons** - Comparative analysis of existing job retirement packages versus enrolling in Medicare.
- **Understand the Potential to Enroll After 65** - An in-depth exploration of exceptions and rules you need to be aware of.
- **Penalties** - An easy-to-understand guide on late penalties and its potential financial impacts, including actionable strategies to avoid them.

- **Comprehensive Comparison of Medicare Parts A & B** - Make an informed choice adapted to your unique healthcare needs.
- **Understand Medicare Terminology** - An exclusive Medicare Decoder that breaks down complex terminology into plain language.
- **Real-Life Examples** - Anecdotes that bring the implications of your choices to life.
- **A Step-by-Step Guide** - Organized information that is easy to understand and follow.
- **Highlighting Overlooked Aspects** - The 3 most overlooked aspects of Medicare and how they can impact your retirement.
- **Choose the Best Policy** - Discover if a Medigap policy is best for your situation.
- **Explore Various Options** - A bonus chapter on alternative options, such as Medicare Advantage and Prescription Drug Plans, to ensure all your bases are covered.
- **Your Questions, Answered** - Common and uncommon questions are answered in an easy-to-follow FAQ format for when you need answers, fast.

You might be wondering, "I already have too many Medicare resources. How is this book different?" or "I've read other Medicare books, and they were too dense. How do I know yours isn't the same?" or even "Can't I find this information online for free?"

Such objections are valid. But here's why this guide stands out: We've meticulously crafted this book to be engaging, clear, comprehensive, practical, and, most importantly, updated regularly. Not only are we breaking down the complexities, but we're also offering the most current and relevant insights. Plus, the wealth of real-life anecdotes, actionable advice, checklists, and exclusive Medicare Decoder included in this guide are designed to empower you to manage Medicare with confidence and ease.

If you're ready to gain clarity on Medicare, reduce stress, and secure your financial future, scroll up and click the **"Add to Cart"** button now! Save yourself and your loved ones, from the hassle and the worry. It's time to proceed with confidence.

introduction

Imagine the following scenario. You're about to turn 65 and plan to retire. You know you'll no longer have a health insurer through your employer and are worried about future health care costs. You hear about Medicare, which offers a great solution for those in your position. However, when you investigate how it works, you may feel that Medicare might give you more headaches than resolutions. It's a complex system with many intricacies most people have a hard time navigating.

This scenario is much like what millions of Americans who rely on the Medicare system face. The disabled and those above 65 feel they have to jump through hoops before they become covered under Medicare. This book was born out of a similar experience but also of necessity for a beacon of clarity in the Medicare maze.

Seeing my 65-year-old mother struggle with understanding how the Medicare system works, I was inspired to create a guide for those facing similar dilemmas. What began as a strong desire to help my mother led me down a path of dedication to simplifying Medicare for disabled adults and seniors. After diving into the Medicare system and assisting my mother in gaining medical coverage and secondary insurance for her retirement years, I helped others in my community, establishing an incredibly rewarding career path as a Medicare-enrolling consultant. By 2024, I had successfully assisted seniors in navigating the complexities of enrolling in Medicare after retirement. I believe every senior has the right to access healthcare without financial strain, and every time I help someone, I know I can make a meaningful difference in their life. Ever grateful for the opportunity to serve my community and other adults and seniors across the country, I wish to help more people through this book.

This book provides step-by-step instructions for applying for coverage to clarify the intricacies of Medicare. It answers common questions, helping ease the minds of those concerned about applying for Medicare coverage and having their healthcare costs covered after retirement or disability.

Little could be scarier than facing financial hardships because you don't understand how to get the necessary help for your healthcare cost coverage. For the same reason, this book will demystify Medicare, making it more accessible to everyone.

The book structure covers everything from basic steps to complicated processes in the following layout:

- **The Foundations of Medicare:** It will help you understand what's covered under Medicare and why coverage matters.
- **Decoding Medicare Parts:** Medicare is a complex system comprising several parts encoded in plan letters. Besides clarifying the concept, you'll also receive tips on how to choose plans.
- **The Right Time to Enroll:** Knowing when and how to enroll and understanding how to bridge gaps in your coverage is crucial.
- **Understanding Medicare Costs:** You'll receive guidance on what you'll be required to pay, including premiums, deductibles, copays, prescription drug coverage, and hidden costs.
- **Avoiding Late Penalties:** Timing is everything in all Medicare plans.
- **Saving Money with Medigap:** You'll learn how to determine whether supplemental insurance is right for you.
- **Financial Assistance and Future Healthcare Costs with Medicare:** You'll explore options for gaining additional financial aid and covering potential future healthcare costs while on Medicare.
- **Medicare for Couples:** You'll learn how couples can coordinate benefits and maximize savings based on age, employment status, health, and more.
- **Navigating Medicare with Pre-existing Conditions:** Understand Medicare coverage for pre-existing coverage.

- **Understanding What to Do When You're Late to Medicare:** This includes strategies to enroll after 65 without penalties while still working and after retirement.
- **Covering Special Circumstances:** Information about Medicare for veterans and federal employees and travel coverage.
- **Everything You Need to Know about Telehealth:** What it covers, recent and future innovations, and staying informed.
- **Comprehensive Guidance for Medicare Enrollment:** You'll receive easy-to-follow step-by-step guidance for enrolling and preparing for enrollment online, in person, or by phone.
- **Renewing and Changing Your Medicare Plan:** Understanding how to switch plans will help you navigate this process seamlessly.
- **Using Technology and Information to Manage Your Medicare Plan:** Besides staying on top of your current plan, you'll also receive resources for continuous learning and staying up to date with future innovations and their implications on your healthcare plan.
- **Building Your Healthcare Team:** Finding Medicare-approved providers is a concern for many. You'll learn how to advocate for getting help and leverage your resources.
- **Additional Guidance on Maximizing Your Healthcare Benefits:** This includes lifestyle changes for retirement planning, preventative care, and preparing for health crises.

- **The Mental Health Coverage of Medicare:** You'll learn what is included and how to receive counseling and support if needed.
- **Insider Tips for Reducing Out-of-Pocket Expenses:** Regularly reviewing your healthcare needs and current Medicare plans will ensure you won't pay more than you need out-of-pocket.
- **Instructions for Other Special Circumstances:** This includes leveraging care during home or hospital care, the costs of alternative medicine, finding niche strategies for different groups, and more.

Besides giving you a precise roadmap for navigating the Medicare layout, the book provides real-life examples. Reading it, you'll encounter various scenarios and anecdotes to illustrate the different concepts more vividly, enabling you to see yourself in the scenarios and understand how to put the information into practice.

Shopping for health insurance without understanding the process can be intimidating. With the amount of misinformation, steps, potential language, and cultural barriers crowding the Medicare landscape, it's understandable if you are anxious about making the right choices. This book will guide you safely on your journey.

Another benefit of reading this book is the resources for learning more about Medicare. Remember, Medicare is a dynamic system that changes constantly, so staying updated with information to maximize the benefits you gain from it is crucial.

When reading this book, remember to keep an open mind and use all the information as guidance for gaining coverage and as a tool for empowering your future healthcare journey. Immerse yourself fully and take your time to contemplate everything you've learned, including the lessons from the real-life examples.

Thank you so much for embarking on this journey with me. As always, I take pride in empowering communities to navigate Medicare as I believe that together, we can create a better future for retirement healthcare planning. Feel free to share what you learn from this book with others to help them achieve the peace of mind you're about to gain.

1
navigating the medicare maze

Understanding Medicare can be daunting and can seem complicated for several reasons. Firstly, Medicare is a complex program with different parts and plans, each with distinct purposes. You might have encountered terms like Medicare Part A, Part B, Part C (Medicare Advantage), and Part D, each containing too many details that become confusing. These parts cover hospital stays, doctor visits, prescription drugs, etc.

Besides learning about different plans, you must know how to deal with the intricacies of eligibility criteria and enrollment periods. Eligibility depends on factors like age, disability status, and sometimes your employment history or spouse's. Knowing about these enrollment deadlines is critical, as they lead to penalties and coverage gaps, adding another layer of complexity.

Furthermore, Medicare policies and regulations can undergo frequent updates and revisions, making staying up to date with the latest changes challenging. There's always a chance that last year's policies might be revised today, leaving you uncertain about your coverage options and benefits.

Another aspect that increases Medicare's complexity is the abundance of plan choices available. While options are beneficial, comparing plans, deciphering coverage details, and assessing costs can be overwhelming. Factors like premiums, deductibles, copayments, and coinsurance vary among plans, further complicating the decision-making process. It's also necessary to understand how Medicare interacts with other healthcare programs like Medicaid and employer-sponsored programs.

From understanding these complex details to deciphering technical and jargon-heavy information, this chapter has everything about Medicare to get you started.

1.1. the foundation of medicare: what it covers and why it matters

Understanding Medicare's Core

Foundational Coverage

Medicare is a vital component of senior healthcare, providing coverage for essential medical services. It addresses three main areas: hospital visits, medical services, and prescription drugs. These components form the backbone of Medicare's coverage, ensuring you can access necessary care without overwhelming financial burdens.

Medicare Part A: Hospital Visits

Medicare Part A is often called hospital insurance. It primarily covers inpatient care, including hospital stays, home health services, etc. Part A ensures financial protection when you require hospitalization for emergencies, surgeries, or other medical needs. This coverage is crucial for providing peace of mind and ensuring access to essential medical services without worrying about excessive costs.

Part A also covers meals, nursing care, and medications administered during a hospital stay. It includes coverage for skilled nursing facility care for rehabilitation following a hospital stay, hospice care for people with terminal illnesses, and limited home health services for those who are home-bound and need skilled nursing care or therapy.

Medicare Part B: Medical Services

Medicare Part B supports Part A by focusing on outpatient services and medical supplies. It covers a wide range of services, including doctor visits, preventive care, lab tests, outpatient surgeries, ambulance services, and providing medical equipment like wheelchairs and walkers.

Part B also includes screenings for conditions like cancer, diabetes, and cardiovascular disease, vaccinations, and counseling to promote healthy lifestyles. These preventive services are essential for detecting health issues early and preventing the onset of more severe conditions, ultimately improving health outcomes and reducing healthcare costs in the long run.

Medicare Part D: Prescription Drugs

Medicare Part D covers prescription drugs, filling a significant gap in Medicare's coverage. It allows enrolled people to afford the medications to manage chronic conditions, treat acute illnesses, and maintain their health and quality of life. Part D plans are offered by private insurance companies approved by Medicare and covering medications, formularies, premiums, deductibles, and copayments.

Part D plans typically cover a broad range of prescription drugs, including medications for chronic conditions like diabetes, hypertension, arthritis, and acute conditions like infections and pain management. Some Part D plans offer coverage for vaccines, insulin, and certain over-the-counter medications with a prescription.

Understanding the core components of Medicare is crucial for you and your caregivers to make informed decisions about healthcare coverage. While these parts cover many essential services, it's necessary to be aware of potential coverage gaps and consider supplemental insurance options like Medigap plans or Medicare Advantage to enhance coverage and provide additional benefits.

The Importance of Coverage

As you age, you may encounter various medical needs and expenses. With Medicare coverage, you can achieve financial protection against unexpected health issues, making access to healthcare more accessible and affordable. Medicare is like a safety net, offering financial protection against the high costs of healthcare services. Without Medicare coverage, you could face significant financial strain when dealing with medical emergencies, hospital stays, or chronic conditions. Medicare helps alleviate this burden by covering healthcare expenses, including hospital visits, medical services, and prescription drugs, reducing out-of-pocket costs for you and your family.

If you have a fixed income, dealing with medical emergencies and serious illnesses can lead to excessive healthcare costs, potentially causing financial hardship. Medicare helps you avoid catastrophic expenses from surgeries to medications depleting your savings or retirement funds.

Medicare is a lifeline for millions of Americans, offering peace of mind, security, and support as they navigate the complexities of aging and healthcare. It is the key to safeguarding your health and well-being, promoting independence, and enhancing quality of life in later years.

Coverage Limits

While Medicare provides essential coverage for many healthcare services, you must know what it does not cover. Recognizing these coverage limits is necessary to opt for supplemental plans and receive the comprehensive care you need.

Here's what Medicare typically does not cover:

Long-Term Care

One significant limitation of Medicare is its lack of coverage for long-term care services like daily living assistance (e.g., bathing, dressing, and eating) in a nursing home or assisted living facility. Medicare Part A may cover short-term stays in skilled nursing facilities for rehabilitation following a hospital stay. Still, it does not provide coverage for ongoing assistance with daily activities.

Dental Care

Medicare does not cover routine dental care, including cleanings, fillings, extractions, or dentures. While some exceptions for dental services are integral to covered medical procedures (e.g., jaw reconstruction following an injury), routine dental care is typically not covered under Medicare.

Vision Care

Similarly, Medicare does not cover routine vision care like eye exams for prescription glasses or contact lenses. While Medicare may cover specific eye exams for diagnosing and treating eye diseases (e.g., glaucoma or macular degeneration), routine vision exams and corrective lenses are generally not covered.

Hearing Aids

The costs of hearing aids or routine diagnostic hearing exams for hearing loss are not facilitated unless a doctor requests them to diagnose or treat a medical condition.

Cosmetic Procedures

You won't get coverage for cosmetic procedures or treatments performed solely for aesthetic purposes. These include elective surgeries, cosmetic injections (e.g., Botox), and other aesthetic treatments intended to alter appearance rather than treat a medical condition.

Prescription Drugs (in Some Cases)

While Medicare Part D covers prescription drugs, not all medications are covered. Each Part D plan has its formulary, listing the specific drugs it covers. Some drugs may be excluded from coverage, or there may be restrictions on coverage based on dosage, frequency, or medical necessity.

The Need for Supplemental Plans

Many people enroll in supplemental insurance plans to fill the gaps in Medicare coverage. A prime example is the Medigap plan, or Medicare Supplement Insurance, which helps cover out-of-pocket costs. Similarly, Medicare Advantage plans (Part C) will be the right choice to secure dental coverage and hearing care.

The Role of Medicare in Retirement Planning

Retirement Age Considerations

Medicare eligibility at 65 significantly influences decisions about when to retire. For many, this age is a benchmark for transitioning from employer-sponsored health insurance to Medicare coverage. Delaying retirement until age 65 or later helps avoid gaps in healthcare coverage and potential penalties for late enrollment. Conversely, retiring before age 65 may necessitate interim health insurance coverage, like the COBRA (Consolidated Omnibus Budget Reconciliation Act), for health coverage in a group or private plan until Medicare eligibility begins.

Healthcare Costs and Savings Strategies

Understanding potential healthcare costs in retirement is essential to implementing saving strategies, including factoring in deductibles, copayments, and premiums for supplemental insurance plans. Although you can avail yourself of Medicare or Medicaid, saving before retirement for results is better. Some effective strategies include saving diligently in retirement accounts like 401(k)s, IRAs, and HSAs to help cover healthcare expenses not included in basic Medicare coverage. Supplementary insurance options like Medigap or Medicare Advantage can provide additional coverage and financial protection.

Proactively addressing healthcare costs and coverage gaps can help you adjust your savings goals, investment strategies, and retirement timelines accordingly.

1.2. decoding medicare parts: a deep dive into parts a, b, c, and d

Breakdown of Benefits

Medicare comprises parts, each with a distinct purpose and covering various healthcare needs. Understanding these parts' benefits is crucial for comprehensive coverage in different healthcare scenarios.

Medicare Part A: Hospital Insurance

- **Hospital Stays:** Covers most areas of inpatient care in hospitals. It includes on-request provision of semiprivate rooms, meals, general nursing, and other hospital services and supplies.
- **Skilled Nursing Facility Care:** You will get coverage for skilled nursing care and rehabilitation services in a skilled nursing facility.
- **Hospice Care:** This plan offers coverage for palliative care for terminally ill patients, including medical, social, and support services.
- **Home Health Services:** Includes part-time or intermittent skilled nursing care, home health aide services, physical therapy, occupational therapy, and speech-language pathology services.

Medicare Part B: Medical Insurance

Doctor Visits: Covers medically necessary services, doctors, and other healthcare providers, including outpatient care and preventive services.

Outpatient Care: Includes services like lab tests, X-rays, ambulance services, and durable medical equipment.

Preventive Services: This plan provides coverage for screenings, vaccines, and counseling to prevent or detect illnesses at an early stage.

Home Health Services: Covers part-time or intermittent skilled nursing care, physical therapy, occupational therapy, and speech-language pathology services.

Medicare Part C: Medicare Advantage Plans

This plan offers all benefits and services covered under Parts A and B, usually through private insurance companies approved by Medicare. It may include additional benefits not covered by original Medicare like vision, dental, hearing, and prescription drug coverage.

Medicare Part D: Prescription Drug Coverage

Covers prescription drugs, helping to lower medication costs and ensure access to necessary treatments. It's available through private insurance companies approved by Medicare. It helps with prescription drug payments through stand-alone prescription drug plans (PDPs) or Medicare Advantage plans with prescription drug coverage (MA-PDs).

Understanding the breakdown of benefits provided by each Medicare part makes knowing your healthcare coverage needs easier and choosing the right plan for comprehensive care.

Choosing the Right Combination

Here's a guide on how to navigate this decision-making process effectively:

Evaluate Healthcare Needs

Begin by assessing your current health status and anticipated healthcare needs. Consider factors like chronic conditions or ongoing illnesses. If it's too complicated, visit your doctor to learn about your medical issues, prescription medications, and the expected frequency of visits for better management.

For example, if you have frequent doctor visits and require ongoing medical care, comprehensive coverage with Medicare Parts A, B, and D may be suitable.

Assess Financial Situation

Evaluate your financial situation, including income, savings, and budget. Determine how much you can pay in premiums, deductibles, and out-of-pocket expenses. Compare the costs associated with different Medicare parts and evaluate how these costs align with your budget and financial goals.

Consider Individual Preferences

Consider your preferences regarding healthcare providers, prescription drug coverage, and access to additional benefits. Determine whether you prefer the flexibility of original Medicare (Parts A and B) or the convenience of Medicare Advantage plans, which often include prescription drug coverage and additional benefits like dental and vision care.

Seek Professional Guidance

Consult a licensed insurance agent or Medicare counselor for personalized guidance and assistance in selecting the right combination of Medicare parts based on your needs and circumstances. Furthermore, take advantage of resources such as Medicare.gov, which offers tools and resources to help you compare plans, estimate costs, and make informed decisions about your healthcare coverage.

Understanding Premiums and Deductibles

Navigating the costs associated with each Medicare part is crucial for effective healthcare budgeting. Here's a breakdown of premiums and deductibles to help you plan for healthcare expenses:

Medicare Part A: Hospital Insurance

Most people do not pay a premium for Part A if they or their spouse paid Medicare taxes while working. Suppose you aren't eligible for premium-free Part A. In that case, you can purchase coverage, with the premium depending on your work history. Part A has a deductible for hospital stays covering the first 60 days of inpatient care per benefit period.

Medicare Part B: Medical Insurance

Part B has a standard monthly premium, adjusted annually based on income. Additionally, you must meet an annual deductible for Part B before Medicare starts paying its share of covered services. For the majority of medical treatments, durable medical equipment, and outpatient therapy, one normally pays 20% of the Medicare-approved price after fulfilling the deductible.

Medicare Part C: Medicare Advantage Plans

Premiums for Medicare Advantage plans vary depending on the plan. Still, they typically include the Part B premium and an additional premium. Some plans have deductibles and cost-sharing requirements for covered services, like copayments or coinsurance for doctor visits and hospital stays.

Medicare Part D: Prescription Drug Coverage

Part D prescription drug plans have monthly premiums, which vary depending on your plan and location. In addition to the premium, you may also have an annual deductible for prescription drugs, depending on the plan. After meeting the deductible, you pay copayment or coinsurance for each prescription, and the plan covers the remaining cost.

The Importance of Part D

Part D prescription drug coverage is crucial in managing health and reducing healthcare expenses for Medicare beneficiaries. Here's why Part D is essential:

Part D provides access to various prescription medications, including managing chronic conditions, treating acute illnesses, and preventing disease progression. Coverage for prescription drugs ensures you can afford your medications to maintain your health.

Furthermore, prescription drugs can be expensive, particularly for people with chronic conditions requiring multiple medications. Part D provides financial protection by helping offset prescription drug costs, reducing out-of-pocket expenses for Medicare beneficiaries, and easing the economic burden of medication costs.

Access to affordable prescription medications leads to cost savings across the healthcare system by preventing more expensive medical interventions like hospitalizations and emergency room visits.

1.3. the alphabet soup of medicare: making sense of plan letters

Demystifying Plan Options

For Medicare beneficiaries seeking supplemental coverage to complement Original Medicare, understanding the differences between Medigap plans, from Plan A to Plan N, is essential. Here's a breakdown of the various Medigap plans and how they complement Original Medicare:

Plan A: Offers basic coverage, including Medicare Part A coinsurance and hospital costs up to an additional 365 days after Medicare benefits are exhausted, as well as Medicare Part B coinsurance or copayments.

Plan B: Includes the same benefits as Plan A, plus coverage for the Medicare Part A deductible.

Plan C: Provides comprehensive coverage, including all benefits covered by Plan B, including coverage for Medicare Part B deductible, skilled nursing facility care coinsurance, and limited foreign travel emergency care.

Plan D: Offers coverage for Medicare Part A deductible, skilled nursing facility care coinsurance, and limited foreign travel emergency care but does not cover the Medicare Part B deductible.

Plan F: Provides the most comprehensive coverage, including all benefits covered by Plan C and coverage for the Medicare Part B deductible.

Plan G: Like Plan F, except it does not cover the Medicare Part B deductible.

Plan K: Offers lower coverage with lower premiums, covering 50% of Medicare Part A deductible, coinsurance, and copayments, and 50% of Medicare Part B coinsurance or copayments.

Plan L: Like Plan K but with higher cost-sharing, covering 75% of Medicare Part A deductible, coinsurance, and copayments, and 75% of Medicare Part B coinsurance or copayments.

Plan M: Provides coverage like Plan D but with lower premiums, covering 50% of the Medicare Part A deductible and skilled nursing facility care coinsurance.

Plan N: Offers coverage for Medicare Part A deductible, skilled nursing facility care coinsurance, and limited foreign travel emergency care, with copayments for specific office and emergency room visits.

Each Medigap plan offers different coverage levels, allowing people to choose the one that best meets their healthcare needs and budget.

Tailoring Coverage to Your Needs

As you did earlier when selecting the right Medicare combination, start by evaluating your health, reviewing the available coverage options, comparing plans, and considering budgeting constraints to tailor the coverage to receive the maximum benefits. Furthermore, it would help if you considered factors like prescription medication requirements, frequency of doctor visits, and upcoming medical procedures or treatments.

Comparing Medigap Plans

When comparing Medigap plans, evaluating the benefits and costs of each plan to determine which option best meets your needs is essential. Here's a strategy for comparing plans effectively:

Start by reviewing the essential benefits covered by all Medigap plans. Then, identify additional benefits specific Medigap plans offer beyond the basic coverage. This may include coverage for the Medicare Part A deductible, Medicare Part B deductible, skilled nursing facility care coinsurance, and coverage for foreign travel emergencies.

The second step is to evaluate the cost-sharing requirements associated with each plan, including premiums, deductibles, copayments, and coinsurance. Compare the out-of-pocket costs you would incur under each plan to determine which option offers the most affordable coverage.

Remember to consider the flexibility of coverage offered by each plan. Some plans provide more comprehensive coverage but higher premiums. Others offer lower premiums but require higher cost-sharing for certain services. Furthermore, choose a plan that provides the right balance of coverage and affordability based on your financial situation and healthcare needs.

For example, a Medigap plan F or G may be a good choice if you have an upcoming medical procedure or regularly change your prescription medication. Nonetheless, the aim is to choose a plan that provides flexibility to adapt to changing healthcare needs in the long term.

The Role of Plan Letters in Decision Making

Understanding each plan letter's specifics is useful when making informed health coverage choices. Here's why the plan letters are significant in decision-making:

Different Levels of Coverage: Each plan letter represents a different coverage level, with varying benefits and cost-sharing requirements. For example, Plan F offers the most comprehensive coverage, while Plan A provides basic coverage.

Standardization of Benefits: The federal government standardizes benefits for Medigap plans, meaning each plan letter offers the same basic benefits, regardless of the insurance company offering the plan. This allows for easy plan comparison based on their letter designation.

Cost Variation: Although the primary benefits are standardized, premiums and out-of-pocket costs may vary between plans with the same letter designation. So, comparing costs and benefits across different plans to find the most affordable option that meets your needs is essential.

Tailoring Coverage to Your Needs: Understanding the specifics of each plan letter lets you choose a plan that provides the right balance of coverage and affordability based on your unique circumstances.

1.4. the right time to enroll: timelines and deadlines demystified

Initial Enrollment Period (IEP)

The Initial Enrollment Period (IEP) is a crucial window for enrolling in Medicare, ensuring coverage starts when needed and avoiding penalties. It typically begins three months before your 65th birthday, includes your birth month, and extends for three months afterward. You can sign up for Medicare Part A (hospital insurance) and Part B (medical insurance) during this time. Please complete your IEP to ensure timely coverage and potential penalties.

Special Enrollment Periods (SEP)

Special Enrollment Periods (SEPs) allow people to enroll in Medicare outside of the IEP if they experience specific life events like job loss or retirement. SEPs typically last for eight months after the qualifying event. Missing the IEP due to qualifying events like losing employer-sponsored health coverage can trigger a SEP, making enrolling in the program promptly without penalties easier.

General Enrollment Period (GEP)

For those who miss their IEP and don't qualify for a SEP, the General Enrollment Period (GEP) provides another opportunity to enroll in Medicare. The GEP runs from January 1st to March 31st each year, with coverage starting on July 1st. However, registering during the GEP may result in late enrollment penalties, and coverage will begin several months after enrollment.

Strategic Enrollment Planning

In strategic enrollment planning, you must time enrollment to maximize benefits and minimize out-of-pocket costs. Here are a few tips for assistance:

Plan Ahead: Understand your eligibility and enrollment periods well to avoid missing deadlines.

Coordinate Coverage: If you have other health coverage, coordinate enrollment to avoid coverage gaps and ensure continuous access to healthcare services.

Evaluate Timing: Assess the timing of enrollment based on your specific healthcare needs and financial circumstances. For example, delaying enrollment in Part B if you have employer-sponsored coverage may be beneficial to avoid overlapping coverage and unnecessary premiums.

Consider Penalties: Be aware of potential penalties for late enrollment in Medicare Part B or Part D and factor them into your decision-making.

1.5. the art of choosing: original medicare vs. medicare advantage

Comparing Coverage and Flexibility

When comparing Original Medicare and Medicare Advantage, consider the pros and cons of each option, focusing on coverage limits and network restrictions.

Original Medicare (Parts A and B)

Pros:

Healthcare providers across the country widely accept Original Medicare. You can see any doctor or specialist who accepts Medicare without a referral.

Cons:

Original Medicare does not cover aesthetic procedures, dental, vision, and hearing care. Therefore, you will pay out-of-pocket costs, including deductibles, coinsurance, and copayments.

Medicare Advantage (Part C)

Pros:

Medicare Advantage plans often include additional benefits like prescription drug coverage and dental, vision, and hearing care.

Cons:

Medicare Advantage plans use provider networks, limiting your choice of doctors and specialists. Furthermore, the coverage may be subject to plan restrictions, including prior authorization requirements for specific treatments or medications.

Considering Health Needs

When choosing between Original Medicare and Medicare Advantage, consider your current and anticipated health needs, including access to specialists. Original Medicare can be a good choice if you require frequent access to specialists or have complex healthcare needs requiring flexibility in choosing providers. Conversely, Medicare Advantage may be suitable if you prioritize comprehensive coverage and are willing to accept network restrictions in exchange for additional benefits like prescription drug coverage and preventive services.

Financial Implications

The cost differences between Original Medicare and Medicare Advantage must be evaluated before deciding. Original Medicare typically has separate premiums for Part A (if applicable) and Part B, along with out-of-pocket costs. Conversely, Medicare Advantage plans often have monthly premiums in addition to copayments and coinsurance for covered services. However, they may also offer out-of-pocket maximums, limiting your annual healthcare expenses.

Long-Term Considerations

When deciding, consider the long-term implications of each choice, including the ability to change plans in the future. Original Medicare allows you to switch between Medigap policies and Part D plans anytime. Still, you may face medical underwriting if you switch Medigap plans after your initial enrollment period. Medicare Advantage plans have annual enrollment periods when you can switch plans. Still, you may face restrictions on plan availability and coverage changes.

1.6. medigap explained: bridging the gaps in your coverage

Supplementing Original Medicare

Medigap works alongside Original Medicare to help cover deductibles, copayments, and coinsurance, providing additional financial protection for beneficiaries. As you already know, Medigap covers out-of-pocket expenses, and each plan offers the same essential benefits, regardless of the insurance company offering the plan. With Medigap, you can book an appointment with any doctor or specialist who accepts Medicare without needing referrals, giving you flexibility in choosing your healthcare providers.

Choosing a Medigap Policy

Choosing a Medicare plan or a Medigap policy requires accessing your current health status, anticipated medical expenses, and specific healthcare needs like prescription medication requirements or access to specialists. Furthermore, compare the plans while considering the additional coverage some plans offer. Lastly, compare the expenses and see which Medigap policy best fits with your healthcare needs and budget.

Enrollment Timing

The best time to enroll in a Medigap policy is during the open enrollment period, which begins when you're 65 or older and enrolled in Medicare Part B. During this period, you have guaranteed issue rights, meaning that insurance companies cannot deny you coverage or charge you higher premiums based on your health status.

However, enrolling in a Medigap policy outside your Medigap open enrollment period may require medical underwriting, resulting in higher premiums or denial of coverage based on your health history.

State-Specific Rules

Some states offer additional Medigap plan options besides the standardized plans available nationwide. Familiarize yourself with the Medigap options available in your state to ensure you have access to the best coverage.

1.7. enrollment periods simplified: when and how to sign up

Navigating the Enrollment Process

Enrolling in Medicare can be daunting, but it doesn't have to be. Here's a step-by-step guide to help you navigate the enrollment process smoothly:

Understand Eligibility: Determine when you're eligible for Medicare based on age (usually 65) or certain qualifying conditions like disability.

Gather Necessary Documents: Collect your birth certificate, social security card, and proof of citizenship or legal residency.

Choose Your Coverage: Decide whether you want Original Medicare (Parts A and B) or Medicare Advantage (Part C) and if you need prescription drug coverage (Part D).

Enroll during the Initial Enrollment Period (IEP): Your IEP begins three months before your 65th birthday and ends three months after. Enrolling during this period ensures timely coverage without penalties.

Submit Your Application: You can apply for Medicare online through the Social Security Administration's website, by phone, or in person at your local Social Security office.

Review Your Enrollment Confirmation: Once you've submitted your application, review your enrollment confirmation carefully to ensure all information is accurate.

Wait for Your Medicare Card: After processing your application, you'll receive your Medicare card in the mail. This card indicates the Medicare parts you're enrolled in and the effective date of your coverage.

Online vs. In-Person Enrollment

There are advantages and disadvantages to online and in-person enrollment methods:

Online Enrollment (Social Security Website):

Advantage: It is convenient, accessible 24/7, and lets you complete the process from the comfort of your home.

Disadvantage: Limited assistance is available if you encounter specific issues or have questions.

In-Person Enrollment (Social Security Office):

Advantage: Allows face-to-face assistance from Social Security representatives, who can answer questions and provide guidance.

Disadvantage: Requires scheduling an appointment and may involve longer waiting times.

Always go with the enrollment method that best suits your preferences and needs.

Dealing with Enrollment Issues

If you encounter enrollment problems like incorrect information or delays in coverage, here are some solutions:

Contact Social Security: Reach out to the Social Security Administration for assistance correcting errors or resolving issues.

Keep Records: Keep detailed records of your communications and all documents related to your enrollment to find mistakes creating enrollment issues easily.

Follow-up: If issues aren't resolved promptly, follow up with Social Security or seek assistance from advocacy organizations or legal resources if necessary.

Utilizing Resources for Enrollment Help

Take advantage of the resources available to help you navigate the enrollment process:

State Health Insurance Assistance Program (SHIP): SHIP provides free, unbiased counseling and assistance to

Medicare beneficiaries. Contact your local SHIP office for personalized help with enrollment and other Medicare-related questions.

Social Security Administration: Reach out to the Social Security Administration for assistance with enrollment, eligibility, and other Medicare-related issues.

Medicare.gov: Visit the official Medicare website for information, resources, and tools to help you understand your coverage options and enroll in Medicare.

1.8. avoiding the pitfalls: common enrollment mistakes and how to dodge them

Late Enrollment Penalties

Late enrollment in Medicare Parts A, B, and D can result in penalties. However, understanding them can help avoid unnecessary costs.

Part A: If you're eligible for premium-free Part A but don't enroll when you're first eligible, you may face a late enrollment penalty of up to 10% of the premium for twice the years you were eligible but didn't enroll.

Part B: The penalty for late enrollment in Part B is a permanent increase in your monthly premium. The penalty increases by 10% for each 12-month period you were eligible for but still need to enroll.

Part D: Late enrollment in a Medicare Part D prescription drug plan may result in a penalty calculated on the number of months you were eligible but didn't have creditable prescription drug coverage.

Enroll in Medicare during your Initial Enrollment Period (IEP) or qualify for a Special Enrollment Period (SEP) if eligible to avoid these penalties. If you miss your initial enrollment window, consider enrolling during the General Enrollment Period (GEP) and be aware of potential penalties.

Not Reviewing Plan Options Annually

Reviewing Medicare plan options annually during the Open Enrollment Period (October 15th to December 7th) to ensure you have the most suitable coverage is crucial:

Changes in Needs: Your healthcare needs may change yearly, so reviewing your plan options allows you to adjust your coverage as necessary.

New Plans and Benefits: Insurance companies often introduce new plans or benefits each year, and your current plan's costs or coverage may change.

Optimizing Coverage: Habitually compare plans annually to get the best coverage at the most affordable price, potentially saving money on premiums, deductibles, and out-of-pocket costs.

Overlooking Additional Coverage Needs

Failure to consider supplemental coverage options like Medigap or Medicare Advantage can leave gaps in your coverage. Although you already have a good idea of these plans, here's a quick refresher:

Medigap: These plans help fill the gaps in Original Medicare by covering out-of-pocket costs like deductibles, coinsurance, and copayments. With supplemental coverage, you may avoid high out-of-pocket expenses.

Medicare Advantage: These plans offer all-in-one coverage, including prescription drug coverage and additional benefits like dental, vision, and hearing care. Choosing Original Medicare alone may mean missing out on these extra benefits.

Evaluate your healthcare needs annually and consider whether supplemental coverage is necessary to ensure comprehensive care.

Ignoring Plan Networks and Drug Formularies

You must check your preferred doctors and medication coverage when selecting Medicare plans. Medicare Advantage plans often use provider networks, so verify that your doctors and healthcare facilities are in-network to avoid higher out-of-pocket costs for out-of-network care. Furthermore, Medicare Part D plans have formularies that list covered medications. Always double-check that your prescriptions are included in the plan's formulary to avoid unexpected medication costs or restrictions.

1.9. preparing for the unexpected: medicare and emergency situations

Emergency Coverage Under Medicare

Medicare Part A: Covers emergency room visits, ambulance services, and inpatient hospital care for emergency medical conditions.

Medicare Part B: Covers emergency room visits, ambulance services, and outpatient medical care for emergency conditions, including doctor visits, diagnostic tests, and certain medical supplies.

Traveling with Medicare

When traveling within the U.S. or internationally, Medicare coverage works differently depending on your destination:

Within the U.S., Medicare coverage remains the same regardless of where you travel. You can access emergency services and urgent care at any Medicare-participating facility.

Internationally: Original Medicare generally does not cover healthcare services received outside of the U.S. and its territories, with a few exceptions like emergency care in Canada or Mexico immediately adjacent to the U.S. Still, some Medicare Advantage plans offer limited coverage for emergency care abroad.

If you travel often, purchasing travel insurance with medical coverage when traveling internationally allows you to access the necessary healthcare services.

Unexpected Illness and Hospitalization

Understand the difference between being placed under observation status and being admitted as an inpatient. Observation status usually results in higher out-of-pocket costs and limited Medicare coverage for post-hospitalization care. Ask questions, seek clarification about your status and coverage, and advocate for the level of care you believe is necessary for your health needs. Discuss your healthcare preferences and wishes with loved ones, and consider completing advance directives to honor your wishes in the event of unexpected illness or hospitalization.

Planning for the Future

Consider long-term care insurance and advanced care planning as part of your healthcare strategy.

Long-Term Care Insurance: Long-term care insurance covers the costs of services not covered by Medicare, such as assistance with daily living in a nursing home or an assisted living facility.

Advanced Care Planning: Discuss your healthcare preferences and goals with loved ones, and consider writing a living will or healthcare power of attorney to ensure your wishes are followed if you cannot make decisions for yourself.

2
budgeting for medicare

As you approach retirement age, understanding the ins and outs of Medicare becomes increasingly critical. While Medicare provides essential healthcare coverage for millions of Americans, it comes with costs, including premiums for various parts of the program. Budgeting for Medicare premiums is integral to retirement planning, ensuring you're financially prepared for healthcare expenses in your golden years.

In this chapter, you will untangle the complexities of Medicare premiums, exploring how they're determined and what factors influence them. You'll break down the key elements to effectively budget for Medicare, from the basics of premium-free Part A eligibility to the nuances of income-related adjustments for Part B and D premiums.

2.1. understanding medicare premiums: a guide to what you'll pay

How Premiums Are Determined

Medicare calculates premiums for its parts based on various factors. For Part A, which covers hospital stays, hospice care, home health care, and skilled nursing facility care, you won't pay a premium if you or your spouse have paid Medicare taxes while working for at least 10 years (or 40 quarters) - often called premium-free Part A. However, paying a premium may still qualify you for Part A coverage if you have not worked long enough.

Part B covers medically necessary services like doctor's visits, outpatient care, and preventive services, with a standard premium determined annually. This premium is affected by income and enrollment timing. Generally, if you enroll in Part B when you're first eligible, you'll pay the standard premium. If you delay enrollment, your premium may be higher.

Part D covers prescription drugs and has premiums that vary depending on your chosen plan. These premiums are set by private insurance companies offering Medicare Part D plans.

Premium-Free Part A

To qualify for premium-free Part A, you or your spouse must have worked and paid Medicare taxes for at least 10 years (or 40 quarters). If you can't meet this requirement, you can still get Part A coverage by paying a premium. However, even if you qualify for premium-free Part A, you may still have to pay deductibles, coinsurance, and copayments for the services you receive under Part A.

Part B and D Premium Adjustments

The Income-Related Monthly Adjustment Amount (IRMAA) can affect your Part B and D premiums if your income exceeds certain thresholds. IRMAA is an additional amount high-income beneficiaries must pay on top of their standard premiums. The income thresholds are based on your modified adjusted gross income (MAGI) from two years ago. You'll pay an IRMAA and your standard premium if your income exceeds these thresholds.

For example, the standard Part B premium in 2024 is around $170.10 per month. However, your income is above a certain level. In that case, you'll pay an additional amount for Part B based on your income tier. The 2024 Part B premiums for higher-income beneficiaries range from $243.30 to $578.30 per month, depending on your income level.

Similarly, Part D premiums can be subject to IRMAA adjustments for higher-income beneficiaries.

Please remember that Part B and D premiums can change annually, and the income thresholds for IRMAA may also change. Therefore, staying informed about updates or changes to Medicare premiums and IRMAA adjustments each year is essential.

Budgeting for Premiums

Consider potential increases when budgeting for Medicare premiums in retirement. While Part A premiums are generally stable for most people, Part B and D premiums can change annually if your income fluctuates and triggers IRMAA adjustments.

Set aside funds for healthcare costs, including Medicare premiums and expenses you might pay in unexpected hospital visits, to budget effectively. Don't forget that you have options for supplemental insurance coverage like Medicare Advantage plans or Medigap policies, which can help cover costs Medicare doesn't cover.

2.2. the nitty-gritty of deductibles and copays in medicare

Understanding Deductibles

Deductibles are the amount you must pay out of pocket for covered services before Medicare pays its share. Each Medicare part has a distinct deductible.

Part A Deductible: The Part A deductible in 2024 is $1,556 per benefit period. A benefit period begins the day you're admitted to a hospital or skilled nursing facility and ends when you have yet to receive any inpatient hospital care (or skilled care in a nursing facility) for 60 consecutive days.

Part B Deductible: This deductible applies to outpatient services like doctor's visits, lab tests, and preventive care. The Part B deductible in 2024 is $233 per year.

Part D Deductible: This deductible applies to prescription drug coverage under Medicare Part D plans. The amount varies depending on the specific Part D plan.

Understanding how deductibles work for each Part of Medicare is crucial for estimating your unexpected healthcare costs and planning your budget accordingly.

Copayments and Coinsurance

Copayments (copays) and coinsurance are the portion of the cost of a covered service you're responsible for paying after you've met your deductible. Here's how they work:

Copayments: Copayments are fixed amounts you pay for services like doctor's visits or prescription drugs. For example, you might have a $20 copayment for a primary care doctor visit.

Coinsurance: Coinsurance is a percentage of the cost of a covered service you pay after meeting your deductible. Say your Medicare covers 80% of a service; you would be responsible for paying the remaining 20% as coinsurance.

Copayments and coinsurance vary significantly, depending on the service and your Medicare plan.

Managing Out-of-Pocket Expenses

To minimize out-of-pocket costs in Medicare, consider the following strategies:

Take your time and always pick a Medicare plan that covers your healthcare needs, including prescription drugs, if you opt for a Part D plan. Furthermore, review your plan's provider network to ensure your preferred doctors and specialists are included. Take advantage of preventive services covered by Medicare to help maintain your health and potentially avoid more costly treatments down the road.

The Impact on Your Budget

Effectively budgeting for deductibles and copays involves estimating your healthcare expenses and setting aside funds accordingly. Consider contributing to a Health Savings Account (HSA) if you're eligible to save tax-free for future medical expenses. HSAs are available to people enrolled in high-deductible health plans (HDHPs) and are compatible with Medicare.

2.3. navigating the costs of part d: prescription drug coverage

Part D Premiums

Part D premiums vary based on several factors, including the specific plan, your location, and the coverage provided. On average, they can range from around $30 to $100 per month, but this can vary widely.

When selecting a Part D plan, it's essential to consider the premium and every other factor, like deductibles, copays, and the plan's formulary. Plans with lower premiums may have higher out-of-pocket costs for medications. In comparison, plans with higher premiums may offer more comprehensive coverage with lower copays.

Carefully review the details of each plan available in your area, including the list of covered medications (formulary), pharmacy networks, and cost-sharing requirements, to find the best Part D plan for your needs.

The Coverage Gap ("Donut Hole")

The coverage gap, or donut hole, is a temporary limit on what Medicare Part D plans will cover for prescription drugs. In 2024, once you and your plan have spent $4,430 on covered drugs, you will enter the coverage gap.

While in the coverage gap, you're responsible for a higher percentage of your prescription costs. Please note the coverage gap is gradually closing due to changes in health-care legislation. By 2024, you'll only be responsible for 25% of the cost of brand-name and generic drugs while in the coverage gap. Furthermore, these legislations can be revised, so keeping up to date with the laws, regulations, and legislations is crucial.

Formularies and Tiered Pricing

As mentioned in the previous chapter, Part D plans have formularies and lists of covered prescription drugs. These formularies often include different tiers of drugs. The typical tiers are:

- **Tier 1:** Preferred generic drugs.
- **Tier 2:** Non-preferred generic drugs.
- **Tier 3:** Preferred brand-name drugs.
- **Tier 4:** Non-preferred brand-name drugs.
- **Tier 5:** Specialty drugs.

Generally, drugs in lower tiers have lower out-of-pocket costs. In comparison, drugs in higher tiers have higher copays or coinsurance.

Before enrolling in a Part D plan, review its formulary to ensure your medications are covered and understand each tier's cost-sharing requirements. You can usually find this information on the plan's website or by contacting the plan directly.

Reducing Prescription Costs

To lower your prescription drug expenses under Medicare Part D, consider the following tips:

Use Preferred Pharmacies: Some Part D plans offer lower medication costs if you use pharmacies within their preferred network. Check with your plan to see if they offer this option.

Opt for Generic Drugs: Generic drugs are typically less expensive than brand-name drugs and may be available in a plan's formulary lower tiers. Ask your doctor if there's a generic alternative to your prescribed medication.

Explore Pharmaceutical Assistance Programs: Many drug manufacturers offer assistance programs to help lower the cost of prescription medications for eligible people. These programs provide discounts or free medications.

2.4. avoiding late penalties: why timing is everything

The Cost of Delayed Enrollment

Late enrollment in Medicare Part B and Part D results in penalties, which are additional costs added to premiums for as long as you have coverage. These penalties encourage people to enroll when they first become eligible, as delaying enrollment only increases healthcare costs.

Part B Penalty: If you don't enroll in Medicare Part B during your Initial Enrollment Period (IEP) and are not eligible for a Special Enrollment Period (SEP), you may face a late enrollment penalty. The penalty for Part B is an additional 10% for each 12 months you were eligible for Part B but still need to enroll. This penalty is added to your Part B premium for as long as you have Part B coverage.

Part D Penalty: Similarly, if you don't enroll in a Medicare Part D prescription drug plan when first eligible, and you don't have creditable prescription drug coverage (coverage that's expected to pay at least as much as Medicare's standard prescription drug coverage), you may face a late enrollment penalty. The penalty is calculated by multiplying 1% of the national base beneficiary premium ($33.37 in 2024) by the number of full months you were eligible for Part D but didn't have creditable coverage. This penalty is added to your Part D premium for as long as you have Part D coverage.

You must enroll in Medicare during your Initial Enrollment Period (IEP) to avoid late enrollment penalties. Furthermore, suppose you have credible coverage through an employer or union (or your spouse's employer or union). When that coverage ends, you may be eligible for a Special Enrollment Period (SEP), allowing you to enroll in Medicare without penalties.

Exceptional Cases for Penalty Waivers

You may qualify for a waiver of late enrollment penalties in some circumstances. These circumstances involve situations where you weren't adequately informed about your need to enroll in Medicare or experienced other extenuating circumstances.

Examples of situations where you might qualify for a penalty waiver include:

- You didn't enroll because you were misinformed about your need to enroll in Medicare.
- You experienced an error or delay on the Part of the Social Security Administration (SSA) or Medicare that prevented you from enrolling on time.
- You experienced a natural disaster or other catastrophic event that affected your enrolment.

You must submit a request to the Social Security Administration (SSA) with supporting documentation to request a penalty waiver.

Incorporating Penalties into Your Budget

Adjusting your healthcare budget is essential if you're facing late enrollment penalties. Penalties can significantly increase your Medicare premiums, so planning for these additional costs is necessary.

2.5. saving money with medigap: is supplemental insurance right for you?

Costs vs. Benefits of Medigap

Medigap policies typically come with monthly premiums, which vary depending on your plan, location, and other factors. While these premiums add to your healthcare expenses, Medigap can provide significant benefits by covering costs Original Medicare doesn't, like deductibles, copayments, and coinsurance.

When considering the costs versus benefits of Medigap, weighing the potential savings on uncovered services against the premiums for the policy is essential. For example, suppose you require frequent medical care or anticipate significant healthcare services. In that case, the coverage provided by Medigap may outweigh the costs.

Choosing the Right Medigap Plan

To Select the right Medigap plan, you must compare different plans based on cost, coverage, and healthcare needs. Medigap plans are standardized and labeled with letters (A, B, C, D, F, G, K, L, M, N), each plan with a different coverage.

When comparing Medigap plans, consider the following factors:

Cost: Compare the monthly premiums for each plan, considering that higher premiums may provide more comprehensive coverage.

Coverage: Review each plan's coverage, including deductibles, copayments, coinsurance, and other benefits. Choose a plan aligning with your healthcare needs and budget.

Your Healthcare Needs: Consider your current health, chronic conditions, and future healthcare needs. Choose a plan with coverage for the services you're likely to use.

When to Buy a Medigap Policy

Although you have read this in detail, here's a quick refresher. The best time to purchase a Medigap policy is during your Medigap. After enrolling in Medicare Part B and you are 65 years of age or older, you begin the Open Enrollment Period. You have assured issue rights for these six months, which prohibits insurance companies from refusing to cover you or raising your premiums because of pre-existing medical issues.

Suppose you miss your Medigap Open Enrollment Period. In that case, you may still purchase a policy. However, insurance companies may charge you higher premiums or deny coverage based on your health status.

Medigap and Retirement Budgeting

When integrating Medigap premiums and benefits into your overall retirement healthcare budgeting strategy, consider the following:

Budgeting for Premiums: Include the monthly premiums for your Medigap policy in your retirement budget. Account for potential increases in premiums.

Anticipated Savings: Estimate the potential savings on uncovered services Medigap provides and consider how these savings impact your healthcare expenses.

Long-Term Financial Planning: Consider your long-term financial goals and retirement income sources when budgeting for Medigap. Ensure you have sufficient funds to cover healthcare costs throughout your retirement years.

2.6. medicare advantage: cost-benefit analysis

Understanding Medicare Advantage Costs

Premiums: Many Medicare Advantage plans have monthly premiums in addition to the Part B premium that you must pay. Premiums vary depending on the plan's coverage, location, and insurance provider.

Deductibles: Some Medicare Advantage plans may have deductibles, which you must pay out of pocket before your plan pays its share of covered services.

Out-of-Pocket Maximums: Medicare Advantage plans have annual out-of-pocket maximums. It is the maximum amount you'll pay for covered services in a calendar year. Once you reach this limit, your plan will cover 100% of covered services for the rest of the year.

Understanding these cost components for estimating your healthcare expenses and selecting the right Medicare Advantage plan for your needs is crucial.

Comparing Medicare Advantage to Original Medicare

When comparing Medicare Advantage plans to Original Medicare (Parts A and B), it's essential to consider the cost-effectiveness of each option, with and without Medigap (Medicare Supplement Insurance). Original Medicare typically has lower monthly premiums than Medicare Advantage plans but higher out-of-pocket costs. Medigap policies can help cover some out-of-pocket expenses but come with additional premiums.

When comparing the cost-effectiveness of Medicare Advantage versus Original Medicare with or without Medigap, consider your healthcare needs, budget, and preferences for coverage and provider choice.

Factors Influencing Medicare Advantage Costs

Several factors influence the overall costs of Medicare Advantage plans. As you know, Medicare Advantage plans have provider networks, and you may pay more for services received outside of the network. While Medicare Advantage plans may offer additional benefits, the cost significantly increases.

Making an Informed Choice

When deciding whether Medicare Advantage fulfills your financial and Healthcare goals, consider the same criteria to evaluate which plan suits you best:

Cost: Compare the total fees, including premiums, deductibles, and out-of-pocket maximums, of Medicare

Advantage plans to Original Medicare with or without Medigap.

Coverage: Evaluate the coverage provided by your Medicare Advantage plan, including the additional perks you won't receive in Original Medicare.

Provider Choice: Consider if you're willing to accept network restrictions and limitations on provider choice imposed by Medicare Advantage plans.

Healthcare Needs: Lastly, you must know about your health, chronic conditions you face, and your future healthcare needs.

2.7. the hidden costs of medicare: what you need to know

Services Not Covered by Medicare

While Medicare provides essential healthcare coverage for many services, there are several standard healthcare services Medicare does not cover or only partially covers. You already know about these services, which include dental care, vision care (routine eye exams and eyeglasses), and hearing aids. The costs of these services can add up quickly for Medicare beneficiaries who require them.

Dental Care: Medicare does not cover routine dental care, including cleanings, fillings, and extractions. While some Medicare Advantage plans may offer limited dental coverage, you may need to purchase separate dental insurance or pay out of pocket for dental services.

Vision Care: Routine eye exams, eyeglasses, or contact lenses are not covered. However, some Medicare Advantage plans offer vision coverage for exams and eyewear, but you will incur out-of-pocket costs for these services.

Hearing Care: Hearing aids or routine hearing exams are not covered by Medicare. While a few Medicare Advantage plans have limited coverage for hearing aids, you must pay for these devices out of pocket.

Understanding which healthcare services are not covered by Medicare can help beneficiaries plan for these expenses and explore alternative sources of coverage or payment.

Long-Term Care Expenses

Medicare has limitations in covering long-term care expenses such as nursing homes, assisted living facilities, and in-home care costs. While Medicare only covers the cost of limited skilled nursing facility care following a hospital stay, it does not cover custodial or ongoing long-term care services.

Custodial Care: Medicare does not cover custodial care, which includes assistance with activities like bathing, dressing, and eating. If you want long-term custodial care, you must pay for these services or explore other funding options.

Medicaid: Medicaid can cover long-term care expenses for beneficiaries with limited income and resources. However, eligibility requirements vary by state, and beneficiaries may need to reduce their assets to qualify.

Long-Term Care Insurance: Long-term care insurance policies can help cover the costs of long-term care services not covered by Medicare. These policies will cover nursing home care, assisted living, and in-home care. However, premiums can be costly, and eligibility requirements may vary.

Travel-Related Healthcare Costs

As explained in the previous chapter, Medicare generally does not cover healthcare services received outside of the United States, except in limited circumstances like emergencies in Canada or while traveling through the U.S. to Alaska. Beneficiaries who require medical care while traveling internationally will pay for these services out of pocket.

Supplemental Travel Insurance: Some private insurance companies offer supplemental travel insurance policies to cover healthcare expenses incurred while traveling outside of the United States. These policies typically cover medical emergencies, evacuation, and repatriation but are expensive.

Medigap Plans: Some Medigap plans offer limited coverage for emergency medical care received outside of the United States. Beneficiaries should carefully review their Medigap policy's terms and coverage limitations before traveling internationally.

Planning for Unexpected Costs

To prepare for unexpected healthcare costs in retirement, beneficiaries can take several proactive steps:

Build a Financial Cushion: Save for healthcare expenses in retirement by contributing to a health savings account (HSA) or setting aside funds in a dedicated healthcare savings account.

Explore Insurance Options: Research supplemental insurance options like Medigap policies or long-term care insurance to cover costs not covered by Medicare.

Consider Lifestyle Changes: Adopt a healthy lifestyle to reduce the risk of chronic conditions and healthcare expenses in retirement. Maintain a balanced diet, exercise regularly, and avoid tobacco and excessive alcohol consumption. You can talk with your healthcare professional about lifestyle changes to benefit your health in the long run.

2.8. financial assistance for medicare: exploring your options

Qualifying for Assistance Programs

Various assistance programs are available to help people with limited income and resources cover Medicare costs. These programs include:

Medicaid: Medicaid is a joint federal and state program providing healthcare coverage to eligible low-income individuals and families. Medicaid may help cover Medicare premiums, deductibles, copayments, and other out-of-pocket costs.

Medicare Savings Programs (MSPs): MSPs are also state-administered programs to help people with limited financial resources to pay for Medicare premiums, deductibles, and coinsurance. The four MSPs are the Qualified Medicare Beneficiary (QMB) Program, Specified Low-Income Medicare Beneficiary (SLMB) Program, Qualifying Individual (QI) Program, and Qualified Disabled and Working Individuals (QDWI) Program.

Extra Help (Low-Income Subsidy) for Prescription Drugs: Extra Help is a federal program helping individuals with limited income and resources pay for Medicare Part D prescription drug costs, premiums, deductibles, and copayments.

These assistance programs can significantly reduce healthcare costs for the eligible, ensuring access to essential healthcare services.

Application Process and Eligibility

The application process for assistance programs varies depending on the program and the state in which you reside. Generally, it would be best to meet specific eligibility criteria such as income, resources, and citizenship or legal residency status.

Income Limits: Most assistance programs have income limits based on federal poverty guidelines. These limits vary depending on the program, household size, and location.

Resource Limits: Some programs have resource limits, including assets like bank accounts, stocks, and real estate. However, not all assets are counted toward resource limits, and the rules vary by program and state.

Citizenship or Legal Residency Status: To qualify for assistance programs, you must be a U.S. citizen or legal resident who has lived in the United States for a specified period.

Applicants may need documentation to verify their income, resources, and other eligibility criteria. Typically required documents include tax returns, pay stubs, bank statements, and proof of citizenship or legal residency.

State-Specific Assistance

In addition to federal assistance programs, many states offer assistance programs and resources to help residents with Medicare costs. These state-specific programs include additional benefits or eligibility criteria beyond federal programs.

State Health Insurance Assistance Program (SHIP): SHIPs provide free, personalized counseling and assistance to Medicare beneficiaries, helping you understand your healthcare options, including assistance programs available in your state.

State Medicaid Programs: State Medicaid programs offer additional benefits or coverage options beyond federal Medicaid requirements. You must review your state's Medicaid program to determine eligibility and available benefits.

State Pharmaceutical Assistance Programs (SPAPs): Some states offer SPAPs to help eligible candidates pay for prescription drug costs not covered by Medicare or other insurance.

Always research and explore state-specific assistance programs to maximize your benefits and access additional support.

Integrating Assistance into Your Budget

Once approved for assistance programs, you can integrate financial assistance into your healthcare budgeting, potentially freeing up funds for other retirement expenses. Strategies for incorporating assistance into your budget include:

Reviewing Your Budget: Assess your current healthcare expenses and adjust your budget to account for changes in costs covered by assistance programs.

Exploring Other Savings Opportunities: Use the savings from assistance programs to add to other retirement savings accounts or cover other essential expenses like housing, utilities, or transportation.

Seeking Financial Advice: Consider consulting a financial advisor or counselor to help develop a comprehensive budgeting strategy aligning with your financial goals and retirement needs.

2.9. planning for future healthcare costs with medicare

Projecting Healthcare Expenses

To estimate future healthcare costs, you must evaluate premiums, out-of-pocket expenses, and inflation. Here's how you can approach each:

Premiums: Estimate the cost of Medicare premiums based on current rates and expected changes. Consider whether you'll opt for Original Medicare with or without supplemental coverage or choose a Medicare Advantage plan.

Out-of-Pocket Expenses: Project potential out-of-pocket costs, such as deductibles, copayments, and coinsurance, based on your health status, expected healthcare needs, and coverage choices.

Inflation: Factor in healthcare inflation rates, which may be higher than general inflation. Healthcare costs rise due to advancements in medical technology and increasing demand for healthcare services.

Consider using online calculators, consulting with financial advisors, or reviewing historical trends to help estimate future healthcare expenses more accurately.

Considering Health Changes Over Time

You already know that as you age, you may experience changes in health affecting your healthcare needs and costs.

Chronic Conditions: Estimate costs associated with managing chronic conditions like diabetes, hypertension, or arthritis, including medication, doctor visits, and specialized care.

Long-Term Care: Plan for potential long-term care needs like nursing home care or in-home assistance, which can be significant expenses not covered by Medicare.

End-of-Life Care: Consider costs associated with end-of-life care, like hospice care or palliative care, and ensure your budget accounts for these expenses.

Health Savings Accounts (HSAs) and Retirement

Health Savings Accounts (HSAs) are vital in retirement healthcare planning. HSAs offer tax advantages and flexibility in saving for qualified medical expenses, including Medicare premiums, copays, and deductibles. Here's how HSAs can aid retirement:

Deposit More: Maximize the deposits to your HSA during your working years to build a financial cushion for healthcare expenses in retirement. HSA contributions are tax-deductible, and funds can grow tax-free if used for qualified medical expenses.

Withdrawals: In retirement, use HSA funds to pay for Medicare premiums, deductibles, and other qualified medical expenses. After age 65, you can withdraw funds from your HSA for non-medical expenses penalty-free. However, you'll pay income tax on withdrawals that are not used for qualified medical expenses.

Creating a Comprehensive Healthcare Budget

Integrating projected healthcare costs into a comprehensive retirement budget is essential for ensuring financial stability and peace of mind. The following tips can be used to create a comprehensive healthcare budget:

Assess Current Expenses: Start by assessing every healthcare expense you currently face or will be dealing with in the future.

Estimate Future Expenses: Project future healthcare expenses based on future healthcare needs, inflation rates, and changes in health status.

Allocate Funds: Allocate funds for healthcare expenses within your retirement budget, ensuring you have sufficient resources to cover expected and unexpected costs.

Please review and adjust your healthcare budget regularly and adjust it as needed based on changes in health status, healthcare costs, and financial circumstances.

Creating a comprehensive healthcare budget makes planning for healthcare expenses in retirement easier. It ensures you have the financial resources to maintain your health and well-being throughout your retirement years. Regularly reviewing and adjusting your budget will help you stay on track and adapt to changing circumstances. Understanding and budgeting Medicare takes time. Therefore, remain calm and continue learning to make the best decisions for your life.

3
medicare for diverse needs

Medicare caters to many diverse needs, from coverage for couples to delaying enrollment to combining Medicare with other insurance or cost coverage forms. Besides these crucial aspects, this chapter explains how travel affects Medicare, what innovations have been and are expected to be implemented in the future, and how to navigate healthcare in light of the dynamic Medicare insurance system.

3.1. medicare for couples: coordinating benefits and maximizing savings

As Medicare plans are individual, couples cannot share them. However, in some cases, they can combine benefits.

Combining Benefits for Maximum Coverage

There are many strategies for couples to combine their Medicare benefits for optimal coverage and savings. If both apply for Medicare separately, you'll pay the same premium as everyone else. Still, the amount can vary. For example, if at least one spouse has worked, they may be eligible for Social Security at 62, meaning they'll be eligible for free Medicare Part A at 65. When their spouse turns 65, they'll also be eligible for Medicare Part A, even if they haven't worked.

However, a couple's premium is based on how much both parties earn with Medicare Part B. The higher the combined income, the higher the premium. In this case, lowering is the only way to pay less for Medicare. If both spouses work, but at least one is 65, they should consider retiring as this will automatically lower their income.

Medicare C's benefit is covering costly prescription drug charges. Although you pay higher premiums, if at least one spouse has a serious chronic condition, Medicare C can be a great way to offset the costs. It has the same premiums, so you won't have to worry about covering healthcare costs if they suddenly become higher. However, if you want to sign up for this plan, you must do so when you (or your spouse) become eligible for Medicare.

Medicare D offers coverage for prescription medication but has varying premiums, even for spouses on similar plans. Both spouses must meet the deductible before Medicare covers health care costs. If you want to sign up for this plan, you must do so when you (or your spouse) become eligible for Medicare.

Understanding Spousal Benefits

A spouse's work history affects their coverage and their monthly premiums. If one spouse hasn't worked at all or enough on their own, they may still qualify for Medicare after turning 65 based on the other spouse's working history. However, they can only qualify for premium-free Medicare Part A under the following conditions:

- They're married to the qualifying spouse.
- They're divorced from the qualifying spouse but were married for 10 or more years and are currently single.
- Their qualifying spouse passed away after 9 or more years of marriage, and the surviving spouse is single.
- The non-working spouse has a disability (in this case, they can qualify even before they turn 65).

If both spouses worked and paid Medicare taxes for at least 10 years, they'll qualify when they reach 65 separately.

If one spouse becomes eligible for Medicare before the other, they must decide how to proceed based on their employer's policies. Employers typically have different rules about dependent coverage. For example, suppose the spouse eligible for Medicare wants to keep working after turning 65. In this case, their employer may require them to obtain Medicare and stop relying on the employer's insurance. This can affect the employees and their dependents, including their spouse's coverage.

If the younger, non-working spouse doesn't have insurance, the other spouse has the following options:

- Keep their and their spouse's coverage under their employer's plan (if the employer allows this).
- Switch to COBRA coverage for the spouse —some employers offer this option.
- The spouse can purchase individual health insurance until they turn 65 and become eligible for Medicare.

The situation is slightly different if the non-working spouse is older (and hence becomes eligible for Medicare first). If the working spouse's employer insurance covers them, they can switch to Medicare Part A at 65. They'll only be eligible for this plan until the working spouse retires and qualifies for Medicare. Once this happens, it's advisable for both spouses to switch to Medicare Part B immediately, as it will be more cost-effective. After 65, both spouses will have a higher chance of needing more extensive coverage.

If the working spouse is older than 62, the non-working spouse can qualify for premium-free Medicare Part A. However, if the working spouse is younger than 62, the non-working spouse must pay a premium for Medicare Part A.

Navigating Dual Enrollment

Couples who both qualify for Medicare have several options for Medicare. If they're both over 65, they can obtain premium-free Medicare Part A and Medicare Part B coverage, depending on their healthcare needs and employment status. For example, if one of the spouses is working, they can delay getting Medicare Part B and remain on their employer insurance. This way, the couple will only pay premiums for one of the partner's Medicare coverage. They can always enroll when they stop working.

Before delaying enrollment for Medicare Part B, the working spouse should ensure they have adequate coverage through their employer. If they don't, switching to Medicare Part B might be more cost-effective as out-of-pocket expenses can quickly add up.

Cost-Saving Tips for Couples

Couples who consider Medicare Part Advantage plans should consider the coverage they need based on what they already have. If both partners wish to have extensive dental, vision, and hearing coverage (including yearly exams), prescription drug coverage, fitness membership, coverage for medical transportation, and additional health perks, they can consider buying individual Medicare Advantage plans.

Medicare Advantage plans can differ and are often costly, so checking for the services you already have in your Medicare plan is best. You can determine whether paying for Medicare Advantage will be a worthwhile expense for your household by comparing what you have and what you need. For couples where both spouses have chronic illnesses and require regular visits, treatments, medications, follow-ups, etc., this may be worth it.

Couples should consider their budget when opting for or against Medicare Advantage. Besides monthly premiums, you should also look into drug deductibles, copays and coinsurance, in-network yearly deductibles, and in- and out-of-network out-of-pocket max. Depending on the insurer and plan, these can add up to over $1,000. For example, consider how often both spouses need to visit a doctor or get a prescription drug refill. If at least one of you needs these services frequently, this can affect your deductible.

At the same time, if one or both partners are eligible for financial assistance from your state, you may lower your premiums for Medicare Advantage without sacrificing much-needed services.

Another way couples can save is if one remains on the Original Medicare Part A or B plans or Medigap. These offer plenty of benefits and may cover many of their couple's healthcare needs. Medigap policies have varying coverage for deductibles, excess charges, skilled nursing, and more, so ensure you consider all your factors and decide which fits your situation best.

Opting for a high-deductible Medigap plan can further lower your premiums. It could be a cost-effective option if you don't use healthcare services too often. Some Medigap plans have out-of-pocket limits, but after you pay Medicare Part B deductible and go over the out-of-pocket limit, they'll cover all your costs until the policy is valid.

Medigap can save you money on end-of-life care. Opting for a plan that covers the entire cost of these services can give your spouse peace of mind for avoiding financial strain during the toughest moments.

3.2. navigating medicare with pre-existing conditions

Guaranteed Issue Rights

Medicare offers extensive services to individuals with pre-existing conditions, particularly during the Medigap open enrollment period. By 65 (when eligibility for Medicare starts for most people), you will likely develop a pre-existing condition. For the same reasons, these are seen as new medical conditions under Medicare rules, with no bearing on coverage.

The above rule applies to all original Medicare plans and the Medicare Advantage coverage. Still, your conditions can affect your monthly premiums. The higher the care you need, the more expensive your policy will be. The good news? You can get a more affordable policy by enrolling in Medigap (as long as you sign up during the Initial Enrollment Period).

Keep in mind that while Medicare doesn't have a coverage waiting period for pre-existing conditions, Medigap might have one. You may have to wait up to six months before your Medigap coverage kicks in. However, this doesn't apply if you had a creditable health insurance policy six months before enrolling in Medigap. If you had shorter coverage, you'd have a shorter waiting period (the latter is reduced by the period you had insurance).

If guaranteed issue rights apply, you may obtain Medigap without an additional waiting period for pre-existing conditions. Moreover, during the Medigap waiting period, you can rely on Medicare Part A and B to cover the healthcare costs of your pre-existing condition.

Choosing the Right Plan

Medigap and Medicare Advantage plans can differ, although most of the time, they'll cover pre-existing conditions. The only rule is that you must add these to your plan in time. For those who wish to rely on Medicare Part A and B and only need a little assistance to cover the gaps for copay, coinsurance, and deductible costs, Medigap can be an excellent option for previous and new medical issues.

However, Medicare Part A and B don't have the protection of a yearly out-of-pocket maximum, which can cause financial strain if your condition worsens or suddenly acquires a new, potentially life-threatening issue. Medicare Advantage plans can give you peace of mind by putting a cap on your annual out-of-pocket maximum and taking care of other healthcare costs. However, not all Medicare Advantage plans have this feature. Still, even those that don't will cover 50% of Medicare Part B copayment and coinsurance and 100% of Medicare Part A coinsurance.

Medicare Advantage plans can be more rigid than Medicare policies. For example, they may only cover costs at providers within their network. Depending on your condition, you should consider whether you need a Preferred Provider (PPO) plan (has a broader coverage) or a Health Maintenance Organization (HMO) plan (has a narrower network).

Medicare Advantage and Pre-existing Conditions

Medicare Advantage plans cannot deny coverage based on health status, excluding End-Stage Renal Disease (ESRD) in certain situations. Still, even those with ESRD conditions can get Medicare Advantage if they:

- Are diagnosed with ESRD after entering into Medicare.
- No longer have the condition after a successful treatment.
- Join another plan that covers ESRD (like Medicare Special Needs Plan (SNP).
- Lose coverage for their Medicare Advantage Plan in their area.

If you have other preexisting conditions, you can still get Medicare Advantage, as long as you:

- Have worked the required time to receive Social Security.
- Eligible for Social Security based on your age.
- Are the spouse or dependent who either qualifies for Social Security or already receives it.

Managing Healthcare Costs

State pharmaceutical assistance programs (SPAPs) are one of the most valuable tools for managing out-of-pocket expenses related to pre-existing conditions. Funded by the state, SPAPs provide varying coverage.

Your condition may determine which program you can be eligible for. Moreover, some programs are directed to more specific groups, while others have wider applications. For example, if you have a specific preexisting condition, you may need to apply for a program that provides funding to cover the care cost for your condition (if this exists in your state). By contrast, if your pre-existing state is more age-related, you may enroll in a broader program, like those covering drug costs for the elderly and disabled.

Still, in many cases, SPAPs can cover the costs of medications, tools, and services not covered by other Medicare plans.

Pharmaceutical assistance programs are another option for out-of-pocket expense coverage for pre-existing conditions. Offered by pharmaceutical companies, these programs provide medicine at a lower cost or cost-free for those without nuance or who have insufficient insurance. Some companies providing this assistance are:

- Drug Company Assistance Programs.
- Pharmacy Drug Savings Programs.
- Nonprofit Copay and Premium Assistance.
- Patient Assistance Tools and Databases.
- State Drug Assistance Programs.
- Regional AAFA Chapters and Community Resources.

3.3. late to medicare? how to enroll after 65 without penalties

Special Enrollment Periods (SEP)

Failing to enroll in Medicare at 65 may carry penalties. However, if you or your spouse are working and wish to remain under your employer's insurance, you can do this without facing late enrollment penalties. For this, your or your spouse's employers must have a group's insurance available to every employee and their dependents.

You can sign up for Medicare Part A after turning 65 and enroll in Medicare Part B without a penalty when you stop working. Once you lose your employer's health insurance or stop working, you'll have 8 months to sign up for Medicare, the Special Enrollment Period (SEP).

Other circumstances in which you can sign up for Medicare without late enrolment penalties are:

- Losing other non-employer-related coverage like Medicaid.
- Missing the initial enrollment due to an emergency or natural disaster.
- Missing the initial enrollment because you received inaccurate information from your employer.
- Missing the initial enrollment because you were incarcerated.
- Missing the initial enrollment because you were volunteering or serving in a foreign country.
- Having TRICARE.

You may be tempted to delay enrollment if you don't qualify for premium-free Medicare Part A. However, if you don't qualify for a Special Enrollment Period, you may need to pay late enrollment penalties for double your time spent since the Initial Enrollment Period was over. To avoid this, pay for Medicare Part A until you are eligible for the premium free version.

Penalty Waivers

If you qualify for a SEP but still receive a penalty, you may apply for a penalty waiver. You must complete a form provided by your insurance company asking for a reconsideration. You must complete and return this form to the listed address within 60 days of receiving your penalty notification. Send proof that you qualify for SEP (like having previous insurance through your or your spouse's employer to support your claim. You'll receive a resolution on the waiver within 90 days.

You may need to pay the penalty even if you've sent the waiver, as the amount will be added to your premium, and Medicare can disenroll those who don't pay their premiums. If Medicare determines that you've wrongfully received a penalty, it will remove or reduce the penalty — and if you've already paid it, you'll get a refund.

Enrollment Strategies

Late enrollees have several strategies for catching up on their healthcare coverage, including assessing current health needs and potential cost savings with Medicare. For example, if you have a severely disabling condition requiring round-the-clock care, you should sign up for a Chronic Care Special Needs Plan (if it exists in your area). You can do this anytime, but once you enroll, you won't be able to make changes under this SEP.

If you're joining late because you were told your other coverage plan isn't sufficient to combine with Medicare, join a Medicare Advantage Plan. Do this within 2 months of noticing you'll need more coverage.

If you received Extra Help to cover Medicare costs and you've learned that you won't be eligible for it the next year, you can get a Medicare Advantage Plan that provides the missing coverage. You can do this within 3 months of the date you'll no longer be eligible for Extra Help.

If enrolled in a State Pharmaceutical Assistance Program (SPAP), you can join a Medicare Advantage Plan or Medicare plan anytime during a calendar year. Whether you retain or lose your SNAP eligibility you can do this, as it can be combined with Medicare. However, you must enroll in Medicare within the next 2 months if you lose eligibility for SPAP.

If you wish to join a plan with a higher quality rating, you can do it within a SEP, which for this specific cause lasts between December 8 and November 30 the following year.

Case Studies

Despite turning 65 two years ago, Carl opted not to enroll in Medicare Part B because he had sufficient coverage under his employer's insurance. Now 67, Carl is about to retire, so he will lose his insurance and wants to sign up for Medicare

Part B. Having missed his Initial Enrollment Period, he now faces a late enrolment penalty. Fortunately, because he had been working for at least eight months before enrolling, Carl had a Special Enrollment Period and could enroll in Medicare without incurring a penalty.

Carl's Medicare coverage started a month after he signed up. Since he retired at the end of the month, he enrolled at the beginning of the same month so he wouldn't have gaps in his insurance coverage.

Carl would have had a gap in his coverage if he hadn't enrolled right away. Moreover, if he hadn't signed up within eight months of retiring, he would have had to enroll within a General Enrollment Period (January 1 to March 31 each year), and his coverage would only start on July 1. Carl would have had to pay a late enrollment penalty when enrolling outside a SEP.

3.4. working beyond 65: medicare and employer insurance coordination

Understanding the Coordination of Benefits

If you choose to work past 65 and have Medicare and your employer's insurance, you'll be subjected to the primary and secondary payer rules. The payers are the various coverage types.

The one that pays first (up to its coverage limits) is the primary payer. If your bills exceed their limit, the primary payer sends the rest of your bills to the secondary payer. Depending on the amount and your plan, the secondary payer may not pay the full amount left on your bills, either. For example, if this payer is your employer group plan and you only have Medicare Part A as a primary payer, your employer's insurer may require you to enroll in Medicare Part B to lower the costs.

If Medicare is the secondary payer, your primary payers should pay the healthcare costs. If they don't pay it fully, your healthcare provider can bill Medicare, which will pay for it. However, Medicare may decide to recover the payments that the primary payer should've made.

Deciding Whether to Enroll in Part B

Whether you should enroll in Medicare Part B while still covered by employer insurance depends on the size of the employer and the coverage costs. If you or your spouse works for a company with 20 or more employees, it will likely have group coverage. In this case, you can delay enrolling in Medicare Part B for up to eight months after leaving this job. If you wish, you can enroll in Medicare Part A or delay this, too.

If you sign up for Medicare Part B while still covered by your employer's group plan, the latter will likely be the primary payer. Medicare will only pay for what your employer's insurance doesn't. If your healthcare costs are usually low, you could be paying a premium for Medicare Part B without receiving anything in return.

If you work for a company that employs fewer than 20 people, your employer decides whether you should sign up for Medicare Part B. They may not have extensive group insurance, so in most cases, they will ask you to sign up for Medicare, which becomes your primary payer.

HSAs and Medicare

If you are on a high-deductible health plan (HDHP), you may be eligible for a Health Savings Account (HSA). Switching to Medicare can affect an existing HSA because you won't be able to make tax-free contributions anymore. To put tax-free amounts into an HSA, you can only have an HDHP as health insurance. You can withdraw money from this account to cover your out-of-pocket expenses, but you can't put any into it.

You can delay Medicare enrollment to continue to grow your HSA — as long you have your employer's insurance as your primary payer. If you choose this, you must wait to collect Social Security retirement benefits because you can only get this if you enroll in Medicare Part A.

Ensure your contributions to HSA stop at least six months before you enroll in Medicare. After enrolling, you may get six months' worth of retroactive coverage. If you do, you can incur a tax penalty because it would mean you were fraudulently contributing with tax-free dollars when you were already covered by Medicare (even though you weren't).

Transitioning from Employer Insurance to Medicare

Here is how to transition from employer health coverage to Medicare, ensuring no gaps in coverage:

1. Determine your enrollment period.
2. Familiarize yourself with how Medicare works alongside your private health insurance.
3. Decide when to enroll in Medicare (including when to join each plan you're considering).
4. Look into other Medicare enrollment considerations like your income or Medicare premiums.
5. Decide whether you want coverage for long-term care.
6. Consider (and choose) Medigap and Medicare Advantage Plans.

3.5. medicare across states: understanding regional differences

State-specific Medicare Rules

States can implement various rules if they meet the basic Medicare regulations. Most states implement rules to ease beneficiary requirements to adjust their Medigap plans. As a result, some plans may not be available in your state or zip code. Medicare Advantage plans are often subject to location, so researching the plans to ensure the plan you're considering is available where you live is vital.

Moving with Medicare

If you plan to move to another state, you should research transferring your Medicare Advantage or Medigap plans and perhaps new plans available in your new location. For example, if you move to a new address outside your plan's service area, you must switch to a new Medicare Advantage Plan or Medicare drug plan. You can switch plans for two months after you move. Alternatively, you can return to an Original Medicare Plan but may lose some benefits.

You can switch to a new Medicare Advantage Plan or Medicare drug plan if you are moving to a new address within your plan's service area. However, you might have new plan options in your new location.

State Health Insurance Assistance Programs (SHIPs)

Funded by the federal government and employing experienced medical professionals, State Health Insurance Assistance Programs (SHIP) offer Medicare beneficiaries free counseling and other medical services. SHIP counselors can provide up-to-date information about Medicare coverage, enrollment, and benefit choices.

Seniors can benefit from SHIPs through:

- Personalized Counseling Services.
- Enrollment Support.
- Extensive Medicare Education.
- Assistance with Plan Comparisons and Problem Resolution.
- Those enrolled in Medicare Advantage, Original Medicare, and Medicare Prescription.

Regional Healthcare Networks

Regional healthcare networks are another crucial factor in making Medicare Advantage plan choices. They can help you assess plans based on network size and specialists access. Also, they show you how to choose Medicare plans based on your or your spouse's or dependents' healthcare needs.

3.6. special circumstances: medicare for veterans and federal employees

Medicare and Veterans Affairs (VA) Benefits

Coordinating Medicare with Veterans Affairs (VA) benefits can be tricky. For your VA coverage to cover your care, you must receive health care services at a VA facility. At the same time, for Medicare to cover your care, you must receive care at a Medicare-certified facility that works with your Medicare coverage. In addition, VA benefits do not cover copayments, deductibles, or coinsurance payments you incur with Medicare.

In some cases, the VA may authorize services at a non-VA facility. In this case, Medicare may cover the costs instead of the VA. If you don't enroll in Medicare and keep your VA coverage, you will not have health insurance for facilities outside the VA health system.

You can enroll only in Medicare Part A as it's premium-free. Alternatively, if you want to enroll in Medicare Part B, you'll have more care options outside the VA network. You can use your VA benefits to cover items and services not covered by Medicare.

Federal Employee Health Benefits (FEHB) and Medicare

Federal employees and retirees with access to FEHB and are eligible for Medicare can choose when and which Medicare plan to sign up for. This helps them optimize coverage and minimize out-of-pocket costs. You can enroll in Medicare Part A besides FEHB, but you may lose some benefits and have higher expenses.

Choosing Medicare Part B and FEHB is determined by your age, preferences, financial situation, and health status. To make decisions that best fit your particular situation and retirement goals, you should carefully weigh your options, take future healthcare needs into account, and speak with insurance specialists or financial counselors.

Enrollment Decision Factors

Factors for veterans and federal employees to consider when enrolling in Medicare include the scope of coverage and potential gaps in their existing healthcare plans.

Medicare and FEHB plans offer a broad range of healthcare coverage, including preventive and hospital services, primary doctor visits, and prescription drug endorsements. The main difference is with Medicare, you can opt for coverage only for significant medical events with a free plan (Part A). If you're eligible for Medicare and FEHB, you could coordinate both plans and keep your out-of-pocket expenses to a minimum.

Another difference is in the overall plan costs. With Medicare, the costs depend on your plan (for example, Part A is free for qualifiers, while the cost of Part D is income-dependent). With FEHB all expenses, including deductibles, out-of-pocket expenses, and premiums, depend solely on the plan.

Lastly, Medicare allows more flexible prescription drug coverage across the country. Meanwhile, coverage when traveling can be limited with FEHB. Fortunately, you can gain coverage outside your FEHB plan service area by combining the two insurance plans.

Maximizing Healthcare Benefits

By effectively combining Medicare with VA or FEHB benefits, you can ensure you'll fully use the available healthcare services and minimize your healthcare expenses. Here are a few strategies to consider:

- By having FEHB and Medicare Part B, you can enjoy services that might not be fully covered by one program alone.
- Maintaining FEHB benefits allows beneficiaries to gain coverage for prescription drug coverage without enrolling in Medicare Part D.
- After retirement, Medicare Part B becomes the primary insurer, so certain FEHB plans may offer a partial refund, lowering your FEHB premium.
- If you retire before 65, you may opt for FEHB coverage to bridge the gap until Medicare eligibility kicks in.
- If you don't want to leave your healthcare provider, FEHB plans might include preferred doctors or hospitals you prefer to keep using.

3.7. traveling with medicare: coverage beyond your home state

Medicare Coverage While Traveling in the U.S.

You'll have coverage while traveling anywhere in the U.S. with the Original Medicare Plans. However, this isn't true for Medicare Advantage Plans, which, in most cases, only provide coverage within their specific service areas. Some plans will cover out-of-network care but at a higher cost. If you require emergency or urgent care while traveling, your Medicare Advantage Plans must cover your expenses without additional expenses or restrictions. However, if you travel outside the plans continuously for longer than six months, you'll be disenrolled and enrolled in an Original Medicare Plan. Alternatively, you can take advantage of an SEP and enroll in a different Medicare Advantage Plan.

International Travel with Medicare

Typically, Medicare does not cover medical care on international travel, so having adequate travel insurance in place is crucial. However, Medicare may cover your expenses if:

- You're traveling to Canada on a direct route.
- You are on a cruise ship and receive medical assistance while on U.S. waters.
- If the foreign medical facility where you receive care is closer to your residence than the nearest U.S. facility.

Some Medigap plans can provide coverage for abroad medical costs. The same applies to Medicare Advantage Plans. Always check your insurer's policy to ensure you'll have adequate coverage.

Planning for Healthcare Needs While Traveling

Here are tips for preparing for healthcare needs while traveling:

- Research how you'll get healthcare while traveling.
- Purchase travel insurance based on what coverage you already have from your health insurance.
- Bring your prescription medication and a list of them on your voyage (ensure you take the medicine as prescribed).
- Enroll in the Department of State's Smart Traveler Enrollment Program (STEP).
- Check for and monitor travel advisories for your destination.
- Prepare a card that identifies your blood type, chronic illnesses, medicines you are taking, and allergies. Have this information available in your destination's local language, if possible.
- Wear a MedicAlert bracelet if you have serious medical conditions.

Using Telehealth Services While Traveling

Telehealth services are doctor visits through audio and video communication, partially covered by Medicare. Medicare Advantage Plans cover telehealth services but can have additional telehealth benefits. For example, if you're traveling in a rural area, you may have a right to receive services through any means available. If you can't get into a medical care facility, you should get them at your lodging or, in case of emergency, wherever else you happen to be. The same telehealth services may not be available on Original Medicare Plans, so having Medicare Advantage Plans in place is a good idea if you plan to travel to rural areas.

3.8. innovations in medicare: telehealth and modern healthcare solutions

The Expansion of Telehealth

Medicare-covered telehealth services, including eligibility, services covered, and the technology required to access care, have recently expanded. For example, under the expansion of the 1135 waiver, Medicare can pay for the office, hospital, and other visits via telehealth across the country and in patient's residence starting March 6, 2020. This provides coverage for those living in rural areas forced to leave home to receive care beforehand.

Virtual Check-Ins is another innovation that enables patients to communicate quickly with a telehealth-based healthcare provider. For those on Medicare Part B, this includes E-visits, where patients can communicate with clinicians through an online portal.

You can receive specific services through telehealth, including evaluation and management visits, mental health, counseling, and preventive health screenings.

Telehealth Benefits for Medicare Recipients

Telehealth has many benefits for Medicare beneficiaries, including:

- Broader access to care, especially those living in rural areas where healthcare facilities are far away.
- Reduced travel time and cost, which could deter and delay care.
- The potential for early diagnosis and treatment can be crucial for life-threatening conditions.

Other Technological Innovations in Healthcare

Other technological advancements in healthcare, like remote patient monitoring and digital health apps, are now also covered by Medicare. Through Virtual Check-Ins healthcare providers can monitor patients in their homes, provide advice for aiding recovery, and note changes that require altering the treatment approach. The latter is also aided by digital healthcare apps, which help measure vital signs and provide other indicators of the patient's health.

Future Trends in Medicare Coverage

Besides potential expansions in coverage for new technologies and additional ways beneficiaries can stay informed about these changes, other future trends in Medicare coverage may include:

- Changes in Premiums and Deductibles.
- The out-of-pocket cap on prescription drugs will be reduced, making costly medications more available

for those who need them.

- Mental health counselors of addiction counseling and licensed marriage and family therapists will also provide services covered by Medicare.

3.9. the future of medicare: anticipated changes and how to stay informed

Legislative Changes and Their Impact

Recent and potential future legislative changes to Medicare, including funding, eligibility, and covered services, significantly impact healthcare.

For example, due to legislative changes, adult vaccines are now available with Medicare D without additional costs. Likewise, the cost of insulin has been capped at $35, making this crucial medication more available to those in need.

The Low-Income Subsidy (LIS) or Extra Help program has been expanded to cover the majority if not all, out-of-pocket costs for prescription medications.

The option to smooth out-of-pocket prescription drug costs in monthly installments will be available in the future.

Staying Informed About Medicare Developments

Here is a list of resources for staying up to date with Medicare innovations:

- Centers for Medicare and Medicaid Services
- Medicare.gov
- **Additional funding**

Advocacy and Medicare Policy

By advocating for expanding Medicare-related policies and making the program more accessible to everyone, every beneficiary can influence changes in the Medicare land space. Everyone values high-quality medical care, so supporting this by helping the decision-makers see what they can do to improve Medicare assistance is one of the best ways to ensure the system can cater to diverse needs better in the future.

Preparing for Future Healthcare Needs

In light of anticipated changes to Medicare, you must take certain steps to prepare for future healthcare needs. Some of these include:

- Consider multiple plans.
- Research up-to-date information through reliable sources.
- Learn which medical providers are within a plan.
- Learn which prescription drugs are within a plan.
- Consider what benefits can be gained from each plan.
- Look for additional coverage with other insurance options.

4

your medicare
action plan

Preparing your Medicare Action Plan is essential to make informed decisions about your healthcare coverage as you age. Creating a personalized Medicare action plan makes understanding your coverage options, assessing your healthcare needs, and aligning with your preferences and budget easier. Whether you're new to Medicare or considering changes to your existing coverage, a well-thought-out action plan can help you maximize benefits, minimize costs, and enable access to healthcare services.

4.1. checklist for medicare enrollment: your step-by-step guide

Breaking Down the Enrollment Process

Initial Research: Begin by researching Medicare basics, including its parts (A, B, C, D) and how they work. Consider your healthcare needs and budget to determine which Medicare coverage may be best for you.

Gather Information: Gather necessary personal information, like your Social Security number, birth date, and information about current health insurance coverage.

Explore Coverage Options: Review the available Medicare coverage options, including Original Medicare (Parts A and B), Medicare Advantage (Part C), and supplemental plans (Medigap). Understand the benefits, costs, and limitations of each option.

Compare Plans: Use tools like the Medicare Plan Finder on Medicare.gov to compare plans available in your area. Remember to account for monthly premiums, deductibles, copayments, coverage for prescription drugs, and provider networks.

Consult with Healthcare Providers: If possible, discuss your options with your healthcare providers to confirm they accept the Medicare plan you're considering and that it meets your healthcare needs.

Make Your Decision: Based on research and personal preferences, choose the Medicare coverage option that best fits your needs and budget.

Key Dates and Deadlines

Initial Enrollment Period (IEP): This is the seven-month period that begins three months before your 65th birthday month, includes your birthday month, and ends three months after your birthday month. Enrolling during this period ensures coverage starts when you turn 65.

Annual Enrollment Period (AEP): Each year from October 15 to December 7, you can change your Medicare coverage for the following year. For instance, switching plans or adding prescription drug coverage is recommended.

Special Enrollment Periods (SEPs): These are specific times when you can enroll or change your Medicare coverage outside of the IEP or AEP due to qualifying life events. These include moving to a new area, losing employer coverage, or becoming eligible for Medicaid.

General Enrollment Period (GEP): You can enroll in Medicare during the General Enrollment Period if you missed your initial enrollment period, which runs from January 1 to March 31 each year. However, coverage will start on July 1, and late penalties may apply.

Choosing Between Medicare Options

Original Medicare (Parts A and B): Provides coverage for hospital services (Part A) and medical services (Part B). You can add prescription drug coverage (Part D) and a supplemental Medigap policy to help cover out-of-pocket costs.

Medicare Advantage (Part C): This plan offers all-in-one coverage, including Parts A, B, and often Part D benefits. It may have lower premiums but requires using a specific network of providers.

Supplemental Plans (Medigap): Help fill the gaps in Original Medicare coverage, such as deductibles, copayments, and coinsurance. Beneficiaries with Original Medicare can purchase a Medigap policy to supplement their coverage.

Finalizing Your Enrollment

Submit Your Application: Complete the enrollment application for your Medicare plan. Depending on the plan, this can typically be done online, by phone, or by mail.

Review Confirmation: After submitting your application, review the confirmation materials you receive to ensure accuracy. Include details, like the coverage start date, premiums, and benefits.

Payment: If applicable, arrange to pay premiums or enrollment fees associated with your Medicare plan. Some plans require payment upfront, while others will bill you later.

Keep Records: Keep copies of all enrollment documents, confirmation notices, and receipts for your records. These documents are valuable for reference and documentation purposes.

4.2. documents you need for medicare enrollment: a preparedness checklist

Gathering Necessary Documentation

Proof of Age: Medicare eligibility typically begins at age 65, so you'll need proof of your age to enroll. Acceptable documents include a birth certificate, passport, or driver's license. You may need to provide documentation of your disability status if eligible for Medicare due to a disability.

Proof of Residency: Medicare enrollment requires evidence that you reside in the United States or its territories. This can be demonstrated through documents like a driver's license, utility bill, lease agreement, or voter registration card. If you're applying for Medicare while living abroad, additional documentation may be required to establish your residency status.

Proof of Citizenship or Legal Residency: To qualify for Medicare, you must be a U.S. citizen or legal resident. Documentation to verify citizenship includes a birth certificate, passport, or Certificate of Naturalization. Legal residents must provide their Permanent Resident Card (Green Card) or other immigration documents.

Proof of Prior Insurance Coverage: If transitioning from another health insurance plan to Medicare, you must provide prior coverage documentation. These documents could include an insurance card, policy documents, or a letter from your previous insurer confirming the coverage dates.

Organizing Your Documents

Create a Folder or Binder: Designate a specific folder or binder to store your Medicare enrollment documents. This will help keep everything organized and easily accessible throughout the enrollment process.

Label Sections: Divide your folder or binder into sections for each document type (e.g., proof of age, residency, insurance coverage). Label each section clearly to streamline document retrieval.

Use Clear Sheet Protectors: Place documents in clear sheet protectors. This prevents damage and makes it easier to locate specific documents when needed.

Make Copies: Make photocopies of all your documents and keep them in a separate location, like a safe deposit box or digital storage. Keeping backups ensures access to your information in case of loss or damage.

Verifying Information Accuracy

Double-Check Documents: Before submitting any documentation, review each for accuracy. Ensure all personal information is correct and matches the information on your Medicare application.

Confirm Dates and Details: Verify coverage dates, residency, or prior insurance match the information you've provided on your Medicare application. Any discrepancies could lead to delays or issues with your enrollment.

Contact Sources if Necessary: If you discover errors or inconsistencies in your documents, contact the appropriate sources (e.g., previous insurers and government agencies) to request corrections or updated documentation.

Keep Records of Communications: Document communications pertaining to verifying or correcting information on your documents. Keep notes of phone calls, emails, or letters exchanged with relevant parties.

Special Situations Documentation

Proof of Employment: If you're delaying enrollment in Medicare due to active employment and coverage through an employer, you must provide proof of current employment or employer-sponsored health coverage. This usually consists of a letter from your employer or pay stubs showing active employment status.

Proof of Disability: If you're under 65 and eligible for Medicare due to a disability, you must provide documentation of your disability status. This could include a letter from your doctor, medical records, or the Social Security Administration documentation confirming your disability status and eligibility for Medicare.

Proof of End-Stage Renal Disease (ESRD): If you have ESRD and are enrolling in Medicare, you need additional documentation related to your diagnosis and treatment. Medical records, treatment summaries, or a letter from your healthcare provider can confirm your ESRD status.

Proof of Special Circumstances: You may sometimes encounter unique circumstances requiring additional documentation for Medicare enrollment. Contact Medicare or a trusted healthcare advisor for guidance if you're unsure what documents are needed for your situation.

4.3. how to apply for medicare online, in person, or by phone

Online Application Steps

Applying for Medicare online through the Social Security website is convenient and straightforward.

Visit the Social Security Website: Open your web browser and go to the official Social Security Administration website at www.ssa.gov.

Navigate to the Medicare Section: Once on the website's homepage, locate the section related to Medicare. This is in the main menu under the "Benefits" or "Medicare" tab.

Access the Online Application: Look for an option to apply for Medicare online. Depending on the website layout, this will be labeled "Apply for Medicare" or "Apply for Retirement/Medicare."

Create or Login to Your Account: If you have a Social Security account, log in using your username and password. Otherwise, you must create a new account. Follow the prompts to enter your personal information and create login credentials.

Start the Application Process: Once logged in, select the option to apply for Medicare. You'll be guided through a series of screens where you'll provide information about yourself, your eligibility for Medicare, and enrollment preferences.

Enter Personal Information: Fill in the required fields with your personal information, including your full name, Social Security number, date of birth, and contact details. Double-check for accuracy before proceeding to the next step.

Provider Enrollment Details: Answer questions about your current healthcare coverage, including whether you have employer-sponsored coverage or coverage through a union.

Please review and Confirm: Review your information to ensure it's accurate and complete. Make necessary corrections before proceeding.

Submit Your Application: Once you've reviewed and confirmed the information, submit your Medicare application electronically through the Social Security website.

Receive Confirmation: After submitting your application, you should receive a confirmation message on the screen indicating your application has been successfully submitted. You will also receive a confirmation email.

Monitor Application Status: Log back into your Social Security account to track your application status and check for updates on your Medicare enrollment progress.

Wait for Medicare Card: After your application is processed and approved, you'll receive your Medicare card by mail. This card will include information about your coverage and effective dates.

In-Person Application Process

Locate the Nearest Office: Use the Social Security Administration's website office locator tool to find the nearest office to your location.

Please schedule an Appointment. While appointments are not always required, they are recommended to minimize wait times and ensure you have dedicated time with a Social Security representative. Appointments can be scheduled online or by calling the office directly.

Gather Required Documents: Gather the necessary documents for your Medicare eligibility before your appointment.

Arrive Early: On the day of your appointment, arrive at the Social Security office a few minutes early to check in and complete the necessary paperwork.

Meet with a Representative: When it's your turn, you'll meet with a Social Security representative who will guide you through the Medicare application process. Provide the required information and documentation.

Complete Application Forms: The representative will assist you in completing the necessary application forms. Double-check all information for accuracy before signing.

Ask Questions: Don't hesitate to ask questions about the Medicare program, eligibility criteria, coverage options, or the application process.

Receive Confirmation: Once your application is submitted, the representative will confirm your submission. They will give you an estimate of when you can expect to receive your Medicare card.

Follow Up if Needed: If you have follow-up questions or need to check the status of your application, don't hesitate to contact the Social Security office where you applied.

Phone Application Instructions

Applying for Medicare over the phone is another option for those who prefer assistance from a representative. Here's how to apply by phone:

Prepare Information: Before calling, gather the necessary personal information, including your Social Security number, date of birth, and details about current healthcare coverage.

Locate the Phone Number: Find the appropriate phone number to contact the Social Security Administration. This number is listed on their website or by calling directory assistance.

Call the Social Security Office: Dial the phone number and follow the prompts to speak with a representative. Be prepared for potential wait times, especially during peak hours.

Provide Information: When connected with a representative, give the required information and answer questions to complete the Medicare application process.

Confirm Details: Review all information provided to ensure accuracy. Ask the representative to confirm the details of your application before proceeding.

Submit Your Application: Once all information is verified, the representative will submit your Medicare application electronically.

Receive Confirmation: After submitting your application, the representative will provide confirmation of submission and an estimate of when you can expect to receive your Medicare card.

Follow Up as Needed: If you have questions or concerns after submitting your application, don't hesitate to contact the Social Security office for assistance.

Choosing the Best Application Method

Deciding on the best method for applying for Medicare depends on your preferences, comfort with technology, accessibility needs, and personal circumstances. Here are the options to consider:

Online Application: Applying online is convenient for those comfortable with technology and with reliable internet access. It allows flexibility in completing the application at any time and from any location with internet connectivity.

In-Person Application: Applying in person provides the opportunity for face-to-face assistance from a Social Security representative. This option is preferred for those who prefer personal interaction, have complex questions, or require additional assistance.

Phone Application: Applying over the phone is suitable for people who prefer assistance from a representative but cannot visit a Social Security office in person. It offers the convenience of applying from the comfort of your home and speaking directly with a knowledgeable representative.

Consider Accessibility Needs: If you have accessibility needs or require accommodations like interpretation services or assistance for disabilities, communicate these needs to the Social Security office when scheduling your appointment or calling for help.

Evaluate Comfort Level: Consider your comfort level with technology and your preference for self-service versus assisted service. Choose the application method aligning with your comfort level and preferences for interacting with the Medicare enrollment process.

Ultimately, the best application method is the one that meets your needs and preferences. Whether you apply online, in person, or over the phone, the focus should be on providing accurate information and completing the application process promptly to secure your Medicare coverage.

4.4. customizing your medicare experience: tools and resources for a personalized approach

Utilizing Medicare's Online Tools

Medicare Plan Finder: Medicare.gov offers a user-friendly tool called the Medicare Plan Finder to help you compare Medicare Advantage plans, Part D prescription drug plans, and Medicare supplement insurance (Medigap) policies. Users can enter their zip codes, prescription drugs, and preferred pharmacies to receive personalized plan recommendations based on their healthcare needs and budget.

Cost Estimator: Medicare's tool lets you estimate your out-of-pocket costs for Medicare-covered services based on your current health status and anticipated healthcare needs.

Coverage Options: Through Medicare's website, you can explore coverage options available in your area, including Original Medicare (Parts A and B), Medicare Advantage plans, and Medicare prescription drug plans.

Personal Health Record (PHR) Systems

Electronic Health Records (EHRs): Many healthcare providers offer electronic health record (EHR) systems for patients to access and manage their health information online. You can view your medical history, lab results, medications, and immunizations and communicate securely with your healthcare providers.

Standalone PHR Platforms: Alternatively, you can use standalone personal health record (PHR) platforms like MyHealthRecord or HealthVault to compile and organize medical information from multiple sources. These platforms often feature tools for tracking appointments, medications, allergies, and chronic conditions, putting you in charge of managing your healthcare needs.

Educational Resources

Webinars: Medicare offers educational webinars on various topics related to Medicare coverage, enrollment, and benefits. Medicare experts conduct these webinars, which provide valuable information and insights to help you make better decisions. You can find other organizations and resources to educate you on Medicare and everything related.

Guides and Publications: Medicare publishes comprehensive guides, brochures, and publications covering a wide range of topics, from understanding Medicare basics to navigating specific aspects of coverage like prescription drug plans and preventive services. These resources are available online and in print for easy access and reference.

Workshops: Medicare sponsors workshops and educational events nationwide for personalized guidance and assistance. These workshops cover choosing the right Medicare plan, understanding Medicare rights and protections, maximizing Medicare benefits, and much more.

Community Support and Forums

Medicare Forums: Online forums and communities like the Medicare subreddit or AARP's Medicare community are great platforms to connect with peers, share experiences, and ask questions about Medicare-related issues. These forums are valuable sources of support, advice, and encouragement for people navigating the complexities of Medicare.

Local Support Groups: Many communities offer local support groups or workshops tailored to Medicare beneficiaries. These groups provide face-to-face interaction, networking, resource-sharing, and information in a supportive environment. Contacting local senior centers, libraries, or healthcare organizations makes finding local support groups in your area easier.

4.5. understanding your medicare statement: reading and rectifying errors

Interpreting the Medicare Summary Notice (MSN)

Understand the Layout: The MSN typically consists of several sections, including a summary of your Medicare benefits, details of services or supplies received, payment information, and notices or messages from Medicare.

Review Services: Carefully review each line item to ensure it accurately reflects the healthcare services or supplies you received. Pay attention to the dates of service, provider names, and descriptions of the services rendered.

Payment Details: Look for information on how much Medicare paid for each service, deductible or coinsurance amounts you may owe, and outstanding balances.

Codes and Abbreviations: Familiarize yourself with standard medical billing codes (such as CPT or HCPCS codes) and the MSN's abbreviations to better understand the information. Medicare has online resources to help decipher these codes.

Identifying and Reporting Errors

Compare Records: Compare the information on the MSN to your records. You can check appointment schedules, receipts, or explanations of benefits (EOBs) from other insurance plans. Note discrepancies or services according to your records.

Contact Providers: If you identify errors or discrepancies, contact the healthcare provider's office that billed Medicare for the service. They can help clarify the billing or coding and correct mistakes.

Report to Medicare: If you can't resolve the issue with the provider, report the error to Medicare. You can call the Medicare hotline at 1-800-MEDICARE (1-800-633-4227) or use the online reporting tool on the Medicare website. Please provide as much detail as possible about the error and your attempts to resolve it.

Document Communications: Keep a record of all communications related to the billing error, including dates, names of individuals spoken to, and summaries of conversations. This documentation can be valuable if you need to escalate the issue further.

Protecting Against Fraud

Be Vigilant: Be cautious of unsolicited offers for medical services or supplies, especially if they require providing personal or Medicare information. Scammers may attempt to exploit Medicare beneficiaries by offering unnecessary or fictitious services.

Guard Personal Information: Protect your Medicare card, Social Security number, and other personal information from theft or misuse. Medicare will never call or visit you to ask for this information unless you've initiated contact and are speaking with a trusted representative.

Verify Providers: Before receiving services from a healthcare provider, verify they are Medicare-approved and their services are medically necessary. You can check a provider's Medicare enrollment status through the Medicare.gov website.

Resolving Issues

Contact Providers: If you have questions or concerns about a bill or service, contact the healthcare provider's office directly. They can often resolve billing errors or clarify the services rendered.

Call Medicare: If you cannot resolve the issue with the provider, contact Medicare's customer service line. Have your Medicare card and MSN handy, and be prepared to provide details about the problem. Medicare representatives can help you understand your benefits, file an appeal, or escalate the issue for further review if necessary.

File an Appeal: If you disagree with Medicare's coverage or payment decision, you have the right to file an appeal. The MSN includes instructions on how to file an appeal, including deadlines and required documentation. Follow these instructions carefully to ensure your appeal is processed promptly and fairly.

4.6. renewing and changing your medicare plan: what you must know

Annual Enrollment Period (AEP) Overview

The Annual Enrollment Period (AEP), or the Open Enrollment Period, occurs each year from October 15 to December 7. During the AEP, Medicare beneficiaries can change their Medicare Advantage (Part C) and Medicare prescription drug coverage (Part D). Changes made during the AEP take effect on January 1 of the following year.

Evaluating Your Current Plan

Review Coverage and Costs: Assess your current Medicare plan to determine if it meets your healthcare needs and budget.

Check Prescription Drug Coverage: Review your current prescription drug coverage to ensure it includes your medications at an affordable cost. Compare drug formularies to identify changes in coverage or costs.

Evaluate Network Providers: Confirm your healthcare providers, including doctors, specialists, and hospitals, are still in-network with your Medicare plan. Consider switching plans to maintain access to preferred providers.

Consider Changes in Health Status: Evaluate changes in your health status or healthcare needs since your last enrollment period. Determine if your plan provides adequate coverage for new or ongoing medical conditions.

Compare Plan Options: Research alternative Medicare plans available in your area to compare benefits, costs, provider networks, and prescription drug coverage. Use online tools like the Medicare Plan Finder to compare plan options based on your needs.

Making Changes to Your Plan

Review Plan Options: Based on your evaluation, decide whether to change your Medicare plan or prescription drug coverage for the upcoming year.

Contact Medicare: During the AEP, you can change your Medicare plan by contacting Medicare directly or using the online enrollment tools available on the Medicare website.

Switching Plans: If you decide to switch Medicare Advantage or prescription drug plans, enroll in the new plan before the end of the AEP. Your new coverage will begin on January 1 of the following year.

Adding or Dropping Coverage: Use the AEP to add or drop Medicare Advantage or prescription drug coverage as needed. Follow Medicare's instructions to make these changes.

Special Enrollment Periods (SEPs)

SEPs allow Medicare beneficiaries to change their Medicare coverage outside of the AEP under certain qualifying circumstances. Everyday qualifying events for SEPs include:

- Moving to a new area.
- Losing employer-sponsored coverage.
- Experiencing a change in Medicaid eligibility.
- Becoming eligible for Extra Help with prescription drug costs.

To qualify for a SEP, you must meet the eligibility criteria for the specific event. Contact Medicare or your State Health Insurance Assistance Program (SHIP) for assistance in applying for a SEP and changing your Medicare coverage outside of the AEP.

4.7. navigating medicare's customer service: tips for effective communication

Preparation for Calls or Visits

Before contacting Medicare customer service, it's essential to prepare adequately to ensure a productive interaction:

Compile Questions: List questions or concerns to address during the call or visit. Organize them in a logical order to ensure everything is noticed.

Gather Documents: Collect relevant documents like your Medicare card, Medicare Summary Notice (MSN), prescription drug list, or other healthcare records. Having these documents on hand will help provide accurate information and facilitate the resolution of your issues.

Verify Contact Information: Double-check that you have the correct contact information for Medicare customer service, such as phone numbers, website URLs, and office addresses if you plan to visit in person.

Understanding Medicare's Customer Service Options

Medicare offers various options for contacting customer service, catering to different preferences and needs:

Phone: The most common way to reach Medicare customer service is by phone. You can call the toll-free number 1-800-MEDICARE (1-800-633-4227) to speak with a representative. TTY users can call 1-877-486-2048.

Online Portals: Medicare's website provides online resources and tools, including the MyMedicare.gov portal. This secure platform lets you access personalized information about their Medicare benefits, claims, coverage, and more.

In-Person Services: Sometimes, you may prefer to visit a local Social Security office or Medicare counseling center in person. These offices offer face-to-face assistance with

Medicare-related inquiries, enrollment, and problem resolution.

Effective Communication Strategies

Be Clear and Concise: Clearly and concisely state your questions or concerns to facilitate understanding and efficient resolution.

Provide Relevant Information: Be prepared to provide relevant details and documentation.

Listen Actively: Listen attentively to the representative's responses and follow their instructions or recommendations.

Ask for Clarification: Don't hesitate to ask if you need help understanding something.

Stay Calm and Patient: Maintain a calm and patient demeanor, even if you encounter challenges or delays.

Following Up

If your issue is not resolved during the initial interaction with Medicare customer service, it's crucial to follow up:

Document the Interaction: Take note of the date, time, and details of your conversation with the representative, including their name and references or case numbers provided.

Request Escalation: If you are unsatisfied with the resolution or your concerns need to be more adequately addressed, ask to speak with a supervisor or escalate the issue to a higher authority.

Seek Additional Assistance: If necessary, seek assistance from other resources like the State Health Insurance Assistance Program (SHIP) or contact a Medicare advocate for further support in resolving your issue.

4.8. using technology to manage your medicare plan

Online Account Management

Managing your Medicare plan online offers convenience and accessibility. Here's a step-by-step guide to setting up and using your Medicare online account:

Visit Medicare.gov: Start by visiting the official Medicare website, Medicare.gov.

Create an Account: Look for the option to create or sign in. If you're a new user, select the option to create an account.

Provide Information: Follow the prompts to enter your personal information, including your name, date of birth, Medicare number, and email address.

Verify Identity: Medicare requires additional verification steps to confirm your identity, such as answering security questions or providing information from your Medicare card.

Set Up Security: Choose a strong password and security questions to protect your account. Avoid using easily guessable information and consider enabling additional security features like two-factor authentication if available.

Log In: Once your account is set up, log in with your username and password to access your personalized Medicare information, including plan details, claims history, and coverage options.

Manage Your Plan: Use your online account to review your Medicare plan details, update personal information, view and print documents like your Medicare Summary Notice (MSN), and explore additional resources and tools available through Medicare.gov.

Mobile Apps for Healthcare Management

Mobile apps can be valuable tools for managing your healthcare, including your Medicare plan. Here are features to look for in healthcare management apps:

Medication Reminders: Choose apps allowing you to set reminders for taking medications, including dosage instructions and refill reminders.

Appointment Scheduling: Look for apps offering appointment scheduling features, allowing you to book appointments directly from your smartphone with healthcare providers.

Health Tracking: Select apps enabling you to track health metrics like blood pressure, blood sugar levels, weight, and exercise activity. Some apps may sync with wearable devices for automatic data tracking.

Electronic Health Records (EHR) Access: Explore apps that allow you to access your electronic health records (EHR), view medical history and lab results, and visit summaries on your mobile device.

Secure Messaging:

- Choose apps with secure messaging capabilities for accessible communication with healthcare providers.
- Ask questions.
- Receive updates about your care.

Telehealth Services: Consider apps offering telehealth services, allowing you to consult with healthcare providers remotely via video or phone for non-emergency medical issues.

Electronic Health Records (EHRs)

Electronic Health Records (EHRs) are digital versions of paper charts from multiple healthcare providers comprising a patient's medical history. Here's how EHRs can benefit Medicare beneficiaries:

Comprehensive Health Information: EHRs consolidate health information from various sources, including hospitals, clinics, pharmacies, and laboratories, into a single electronic record. This allows healthcare providers to access a comprehensive view of your medical history and make more informed treatment decisions.

Improved Care Coordination: EHRs facilitate better communication and collaboration among healthcare providers by allowing them to share patient information securely. This can improve care coordination, reduce medical errors, and improve health outcomes.

Patient Access and Empowerment: Medicare beneficiaries can access their EHRs through patient portals or mobile apps, empowering them to take a more active role in managing their health. They can review their medical history, lab results, medications, and treatment plans and share this information with other healthcare providers.

Enhanced Efficiency and Convenience: EHRs streamline administrative tasks like appointment scheduling, prescription refills, and medical record requests. This saves patients and healthcare providers time and reduces paperwork.

Privacy and Security: EHRs are subject to strict privacy and security regulations to protect patient confidentiality. Medicare beneficiaries can rest assured their health information is stored securely and accessed only by authorized individuals.

Staying Safe Online

Protecting personal health information online is crucial for Medicare beneficiaries. Here are the best practices to stay safe:

Use Secure Websites: Only access healthcare-related websites and apps from trusted sources with secure HTTPS connections. Look for the padlock icon and "https://" in the website address.

Create Strong Passwords: Use unique, complex passwords for your online accounts, including your Medicare online account and healthcare management apps. Avoid using easily guessable information like birthdays or common words.

Enable Two-Factor Authentication: Whenever possible, enable two-factor authentication (2FA) for an extra layer of security. This requires a second verification form, such as a code sent to your mobile device and your password.

Beware of Phishing Attempts: Be cautious of unsolicited emails, text messages, or phone calls requesting personal or financial information. Medicare will never contact you asking for sensitive information like your Medicare number or Social Security number unless you initiate contact.

Keep Software Updated: Regularly update your devices, operating systems, and apps to patch security vulnerabilities and protect against malware.

Monitor Account Activity: Periodically review your Medicare statements, explanation of benefits (EOBs), and online account activity for unauthorized charges or suspicious activity. Report discrepancies to Medicare immediately.

Secure Your Devices: Use security features like screen locks, biometric authentication (e.g., fingerprint or facial recognition), and encryption to protect your mobile devices and computers from unauthorized access.

4.9. staying on top of medicare updates: resources for continuous learning

Subscribing to Medicare Newsletters

Subscribing to official Medicare newsletters is an excellent way to stay informed about policy changes, benefits updates, and health tips. Here's how you can subscribe:

Visit Medicare.gov: Start by visiting the official Medicare website, Medicare.gov.

Explore News and Updates: Look for a section dedicated to news and updates, often found on the homepage or in the "Resources" or "Newsroom" section.

Sign Up for Newsletters: Here, you can find information about subscribing to newsletters or email updates. Provide your email address and select your preferences for the updates you wish to receive.

Confirm Subscription: Follow the instructions to confirm your subscription. You may receive a confirmation email with further details.

Attending Medicare Workshops and Webinars

Medicare, State Health Insurance Assistance Programs (SHIP), and other organizations offer workshops and webinars with valuable opportunities for ongoing education.

Check Event Calendars: Visit the Medicare website or the website of your local SHIP to check for upcoming workshops and webinars.

Register for Events: Look for registration information for events that interest you. Registration is usually required, and some events may have limited space.

Participate Actively: During workshops and webinars, actively engage by asking questions, sharing experiences, and taking notes. These events often have valuable insights and practical tips for navigating the Medicare system.

Access Recordings: If you cannot attend live events, check if recordings or materials are available afterward. Many organizations offer recordings of workshops and webinars for later viewing.

Following Medicare on Social Media

Following Medicare on social media platforms is an easy way to receive timely updates and tips.

Find Official Medicare Accounts: Look for official Medicare accounts on popular social media platforms like Facebook, Twitter, and YouTube.

Follow or Subscribe: Follow or subscribe to Medicare's official accounts to receive updates directly in your social media feed.

Engage with Content: Interact with Medicare's social media posts by liking, commenting, and sharing relevant information with your network.

Engaging with Medicare Advocacy Groups

Engaging with advocacy groups focused on Medicare policy changes and support gives valuable insights and resources.

Research Advocacy Groups: Explore organizations dedicated to Medicare advocacy, including the Medicare Rights Center, AARP, and the Center for Medicare Advocacy.

Join Membership: Consider joining membership or subscribing to newsletters from advocacy groups aligning with your interests and needs.

Participate in Events: Attend events, workshops, or conferences hosted by advocacy groups to stay updated on Medicare policy changes and connect with peers facing similar challenges.

Access Resources: Take advantage of resources provided by advocacy groups, including guides, fact sheets, webinars, and helplines offering personalized assistance with Medicare-related issues.

Share Experiences: Share your experiences and insights with advocacy groups to contribute to their efforts in advocating for Medicare beneficiaries' rights and needs.

5

enhancing your medicare experience

While Medicare can provide substantial assistance in your healthcare needs, you can take steps to enhance your benefits. You'll learn about digital tools, resources, team building, lifestyle changes, preventative, urgent care, advocacy, mental health, and late retirement preparation tools you can use to improve your Medicare experience from this chapter.

5.1. the role of technology in managing your medicare

Embracing Digital Tools

Digital tools available for managing Medicare benefits include:

- Medicare-related Mobile Apps.
- Medicare Inpatient Hospital Online Look-up Tool —For Medicare Inpatient Prospective Payment System (IPPS) facilities.
- Online Medicare Part D Prescriber and Drug Look-up Tool.
- Online Medicare Physician and Other Practitioner Look-up Tool.
- Affidavits Look-up Tool — For verifying whether a provider has left the network.
- The Official Medicare.gov Portal, where you'll find access to the tools from above and more.

Electronic Health Records (EHR)

Electronic Health Resources (EHR) is a compilation of your medical history. Using them can help your medical service provider track your medication, office visits, and history and manage your healthcare needs more efficiently.

Other advantages of EHRs include:

- **Improved Quality of Health Outcomes:** By tracking your medications, medical personnel can determine how newly prescribed drugs would interact with the ones you're taking. It can also help them spot allergies and avoid giving you the wrong medication.
- **Enhanced Efficiency:** With easy access to your medical records, medical professionals will find it easier to schedule appointments and send

reminders, bill you for their services, and communicate your concerns and inquiries.

- **Improved Patient Engagement:** Your EHR allows insight into every segment of information about your health and helps manage it better. You can communicate with your care provider more easily because you understand what's happening with your treatments, medications, tests, etc.
- **Better Data Security:** In EHRs, only authorized individuals can access your information. Your personal information is encrypted so it is only visible to healthcare providers, insurance agents, and if requested, you.
- **Cost-Efficiency:** EHRS can save money because it allows medical professionals to circumvent paper-based information storing systems, time lost on administrative tasks, and avoid medical errors.

Online Security

Safety perks notwithstanding, maintaining online security while managing Medicare information is always crucial. Here are a few tips on how to keep your data safe:

- **Use Strong Passwords:** Don't use dates and names that can be easily traced back to you. If you're using several sites and apps to manage your information, use different passwords for each.

- **Use Secure Connections:** Only access your Medicare information through a secure internet connection. Avoid public networks and stick to private bands.
- **Don't Click on Random Ads and Pop-Ups:** Sometimes, scanners use tools to mimic veritable Medicare-related sites and apps. These can pop up when browsing. Ignore them if they do, and only access your usual tools.
- **Don't Respond to Random Inquiries About Personal Information:** Government and medical facilities will not ask you to provide or confirm your personal information through messages, emails, etc. Neither will the companies managing Medicare plans.

Telemedicine Services

People with Medicare can now access telemedicine services, regardless of their place of residence or abilities. Those living in rural areas don't have to travel to a more urban setting to access telehealth visits from medical professionals now. This is particularly beneficial for disabled retirees and those with limited mobility.

Audio-only and audio-visual technologies are also available for those requiring them, along with a range of healthcare services from primary care to psychological counseling. Whether you have a physical or mental disability, trauma, or other impairment preventing you from accessing medical care the old-fashioned way, Medicare-covered telemedicine services can bridge the gap between you and the help you need.

5.2. beyond the book: websites, apps, and tools for medicare beneficiaries

List of Resources

Here is a list of resources providing additional support and information for Medicare beneficiaries:

- https://www.medicare.gov/care-compare/?redirect=true&providerType=Physician
- https://www.cms.gov/medicare/medicaid-coordination/states/beneficiaries
- https://www.medicare.gov/manage-your-health/medicares-blue-button-blue-button-20/blue-button-apps
- Mln Booklet For Medicare Beneficiaries
- Medicare Simulator for Calculating Medical Bills
- 1upHealth patient app
- 360HealthSpot app
- Freedom's CMS Interoperability Portal
- HealthSun's CMS Interoperability Portal
- Optimum's CMS Interoperability Portal
- AaNeel Member Portal
- AaNeel Member Portal – Prominence Health Plan
- Achievement Reward Platform
- AgentCubed Platform

User Reviews and Recommendations

When I retired 5 years ago at 65, I didn't have many health issues, so I only opted for Medicare insurance covering basic needs, regular visits, etc. Fast forward a couple of years, and I developed three conditions that now require significantly more care. To avoid paying more or getting into financial strain, I had to learn that I must shop around and compare more options than I did initially. I only wish I had done this as soon as I started enrollment in Medicare. I highly recommend everyone access potential health-care needs for the future when browsing for providers and services in the Medicare network. - Carl, Chicago

Staying Updated

While this provides a foundation for understanding Medicare, further resources can help you stay informed about changes to Medicare policies, coverage options, and healthcare laws affecting seniors, providers, and everyone else in the Medicare system.

Accessibility Features

On the official Medicare website and among the list of resources from above, you'll see many with accessibility features to ensure all beneficiaries, regardless of physical ability, can use them fully.

5.3. building your healthcare team: finding medicare-approved providers

Provider Networks

Once you learn what services you need from a provider or facility, you can search for the best fit for your healthcare needs. The first step is to search for potential providers, services, or medical facilities in your area. Besides pursuing online tools and your specific insurance plan, you can also ask coworkers, relatives, friends, and community members. Alternatively, you can seek referrals from medical societies and other accreditation organizations, hospitals you visited with your loved ones, etc.

If you're enrolled in one of the original Medicare plans, using the in-network providers can bring your out-of-pocket costs to a minimum. Using in-network providers on Medical Advantage plans is an excellent opportunity to reduce expenses.

Importance of Coordination

Having a coordinated healthcare team to ensure you receive proper care is crucial. Working with Medicare-approved providers is a great way to coordinate among your various providers. They need to communicate about your medical history, current needs, and treatment so they can provide the best tools for maintaining and reinstating your health.

Changing Providers

If your healthcare needs are not being met or you aren't getting the proper care, you have the right to change providers. How you do it depends on your Medicare plan. Requirements can vary so it's best to consult your plan for the specific steps required for a provider switch.

With Original Medicare plans, you aren't required to have one specific primary care physician. You can see any doctor within the network. If you want to switch to a primary care provider, make an appointment with a different one. With specialized careers, you may need to fill out a form requesting a change for another in-network carer.

If you have a Medicare Advantage HMO plan and want to change your primary care doctor, contact your insurer to inform them of the change. They'll likely have you fill out a change of provider form. You can call the member services department for help. Your new doctor must be compatible with your plan.

If your plan is a Medicare Advantage PPO, you can consult a different doctor in your network. However, since each plan's rules for switching are unique, contact your insurer to understand their requirements.

Building a Relationship with Providers

Provide tips on building a strong patient-provider relationship, emphasizing communication, trust, and mutual respect. You must build a strong relationship with your healthcare providers to ensure successful collaboration.

Below are a few tips on how to build a relationship:

Prepare for Your Appointments

Make a list of questions and concerns you want to discuss during your visit. This could be a symptom, current treatment, medication side effects, vaccine availability, etc. Ensure to mention anything new, and don't delay seeking help. Voicing your concerns will help your doctor provide better care and establish mutual trust in your relationship.

Bring a Loved One to Your Appointment

Bringing a loved one to your appointment can be reassuring, especially if it's your first visit to a new provider. They can help if you suffer from a serious condition that affects your focus. In both cases, a loved one can mention symptoms and concerns you haven't thought of but could be useful for treating or managing your condition.

You could bring a language interpreter if you're afraid of a language barrier. It will make communicating with your provider much easier.

Be Honest

Another way to establish trust with your provider is always to be honest with them. Ensure to mention everything that's happened since the last visit, from lifestyle habits to unusual symptoms to skipping medication. Every detail impacts your care and relationship with your doctor.

Go Over Your Care Plan

Revise your care plan with your doctor. If there is something you don't understand, make sure to ask them about it. Don't leave an appointment until you have questions. Make a follow-up appointment right away if you do.

Follow Your Plan

Follow your care plan as closely as possible. It may include steps like taking your blood pressure regularly, monitoring your blood sugar at certain times a day, being more active, etc. Ask your provider to reevaluate your plan if there is something you can't do.

5.4. medicare and lifestyle: incorporating healthcare into retirement planning

Long-Term Health Goals

Setting and achieving long-term goals will help you make the most of your Medicare benefits. Here are a few steps to guide you:

- **Be Realistic:** Unrealistic lifestyle changes are not sustainable. By setting reachable goals, you have much better chances of achieving them.
- **Plan the Steps:** Break larger goals into smaller, easy-to-manage steps. For instance, if you need to cut back on unhealthy food, start with something you won't miss as much and slowly work toward foods you enjoy.

- **Be Persistent:** Acknowledge that it's okay to stray off course but get back on track as soon as possible. For example, if you missed a visit or screening, make another appointment to ensure you stay on top of your care.
- **Reward Yourself:** When you achieve a goal, do something that feels like a reward, like going to the movies, buying a small treat, etc.
- **See Assistance for Preventative Care:** Find resources and connect with people who share or will support you in achieving your goals. Preventing healthcare issues is a goal many seniors share, so you won't have trouble finding like-minded individuals.
- **Keep a Record:** Record your progress toward your goals, like every step you took and what you experienced along the way (including symptoms you can mention to your doctor).

Lifestyle Choices

Your lifestyle choices, like diet, exercise, and hobbies, impact healthcare needs and Medicare planning. By implementing healthier and preventative options, you'll reduce your costs and save time and effort in finding the right care and services for your diverse needs.

Healthcare Mobility

You won't lose your Original Medicare, A and B coverage if you move to another state. However, if you have a Medicare Advantage plan or a stand-alone Medicare prescription drug plan, you should tell the plan before you relocate. Typically, these plans won't cover you in another state.

Financial Health

Integrate healthcare into financial retirement planning, focusing on budgeting for out-of-pocket expenses and understanding how Medicare choices affect the long-term financial future.

Here is how to Integrate healthcare into financial retirement planning:

- **Prepare for Long-Term Care Expenses:** These can take a huge chunk of your retirement planning goals because Medicare doesn't pay for long-term care. You can obtain this coverage through a life insurance policy.
- **Consider When You'll Retire:** If you haven't retired and plan to work beyond 65, consider when you will retire. Based on this, you can calculate whether your savings and current insurance plans will be enough to cover all your costs.
- **Estimate Your Costs:** While you can't predict the future, you can estimate how much you're expected to spend. For example, if you have a chronic illness, you can calculate how much it will cost to receive care.
- **Set up a Health Saving Account (HSA):** These are tax-free, so you won't have to worry about inflation and added taxes. You can withdraw when needed, and it is also tax-free.

5.5. the importance of preventative care in medicare

Coverage for Preventative Services

Prevention can go a long way in maintaining good health for retirees. Fortunately, there is a plethora of preventive services covered by Medicare, including screenings, vaccinations, and wellness visits. The scope of coverage for these can vary from one plan to another, but beneficiaries have a wide range of services.

Utilizing Preventative Care

Beyond prevention, taking advantage of preventative care services helps you detect potentially life-threatening medical events at an early stage. As you age, the risks of these conditions increase exponentially, so routine checkups are crucial.

Feel free to utilize your Medicare-covered preventive service benefits fully - you'll invest in your health. Prevention can help you avoid additional costs and unnecessary interventions and improve outcomes for the conditions discovered during routine visits.

Personalized Prevention Plan

As part of your preventative care, your healthcare provider will devise or update your personalized prevention plan yearly. This will happen during your annual wellness visit, for which you can prepare by gathering the following information:

- Names of all your current healthcare providers and their specialties.
- Your current medical records detailing your screenings, immunizations, and past care.
- Family anamnesis (comprehensive health history).
- A list of current alternative treatments, including community-based interventions and self-managed techniques for mental health issues.

After you've provided the necessary information, your doctor will document additional details and discuss potential prevention goals. As part of your preparation, think about potential health goals and the concerns you may have in advance.

Having discussed your goals, your doctor will provide you with resources for additional educational services (and counseling if needed), lifestyle changes, and community-based programs promoting disease prevention, wellness, and self-health management. For example, they may offer physical activity and nutrition referral programs to prevent diabetes, heart disease, etc.

When receiving the referrals, inquire about their:

- **Accessibility:** Whether traveling far or the programs fit your schedule and needs can determine if it would be the right preventative choice for you.
- **Language:** If you require services in a language that isn't English, the preventative program should accommodate this.

- **Availability:** Not all services are always available at all locations. If you plan to move, consider what preventative programs are available near you and at the time it suits your needs.
- **Costs:** Your budget will determine whether a particular program or service is suitable. Besides their actual price, you should factor in transportation costs and other expenses you may incur.

Self-Managed Preventative Measures

Self-managed preventative measures can complement Medicare-covered services like maintaining a healthy lifestyle. For example, physical activity can be a useful tool for preventing and managing physical and mental health conditions. Moving improves blood, fostering better nutrient and oxygen supply, boosting metabolism, and improving cognitive functions like focus and memory.

Maintaining a balanced diet helps prevent and manage certain conditions, lowering risk factors and the need for healthcare services. Likewise, a night of good quality sleep is paramount to your overall health as it promotes recovery, improves hormonal and metabolic functions, and lowers stress. Stress relief is crucial for maintaining and restoring health because the tension can slow down recovery and exacerbate physical symptoms and mental health conditions.

5.6. navigating medicare during a health crisis: what you need to know

Emergency and Urgent Care

Medicare Part B pays 80% of the costs of the approved services for those needing urgent attention but isn't a medical emergency after you pay the deductible and the remaining 20% of the service costs. As an outpatient, you'll be out a copayment for your urgent care needs.

Medicare Part B will cover the emergency department services you'll receive to treat your condition if you have a life-threatening injury or illness. If you're treated within a short period and remain an outpatient, you'll be out of the copayment, Medicare Part B deductible, and 20% of the approved services or items. If you become an inpatient within three days of visiting the emergency department, you won't have to make a copayment.

How much you pay for emergency and urgent services depends on your doctor's rate, if you have other insurance, if the provider is within the network, the facility type, and if you receive a service, item, or test.

Hospitalization

You may be considered an outpatient if you're admitted to a hospital but only remain for overnight observation. This is good news because your status as an outpatient and inpatient status will affect your Medicare coverage and what you'll pay. For example, you'll pay less for lab tests, medication, and X-rays as an outpatient because these services are accessible to those in the emergency department.

As an outpatient, Medicare may cover your observation services (made to determine whether you should be admitted), outpatient surgery, lab tests, x-rays, or other hospital services you receive before being admitted as an inpatient.

Your hospital status determines whether Medicare will pay for your care in a skilled nursing facility. If your healthcare provider officially admits you into the hospital as an inpatient, Medicare Part A and B will cover your costs.

As an inpatient, you'll pay a one-time deductible within 60 days of admission and 20% of Medicare Part B-approved services. Medicare Part A will care for your hospital services (including x-rays, drugs, and lab tests), while Medicare Part B will cover 80% of the services provided by medical professionals in the hospital (including tests, shots, screenings, and more).

All the hospital services (including lab tests, emergency, and preventive services) are covered by Medicare Part B for outpatients, but you'll only have to pay the copayment for each service (the amount varies). This can be tricky because if you require several outpatient hospital services, you may be out more in copays than what your deductible would be as an inpatient.

Medicare Part B covers 80% of your outpatient medical professional services, with you paying the remaining 20% and your deductible.

Regardless of your plan and coverage, you have the right to:

- Get answers to your Medicare questions.
- Learn about your treatment choices and participate in treatment decisions.
- Get a decision about health care payment or services or Medicare drug coverage.
- Appeal certain about health care payment, service or drug coverage decisions.
- File complaints, including complaints about the quality of your care.

Chronic Disease Management

This service may be covered for beneficiaries with two or more potentially life-altering or life-threatening conditions like diabetes, arthritis, or other medical state that can't be fully treated within a year.

With Original Medicare, you'll pay Medicare Part B deductible, coinsurance, and monthly premium. You may qualify for supplemental health insurance, to help you cover your out-of-pocket expenses.

To receive coverage for chronic disease management, you must enter a care plan enlisting your health problems and goals, other providers, medications, community services you have and need, and other information about your health. It must explain the care you need and how your providers will coordinate it. Your healthcare provider will ask you to sign an agreement to get these services every month.

If you agree to get this service, your provider will prepare the care plan for you or your caregiver, help you with medication management, provide 24/7 access for urgent care needs, provide support to get from one healthcare setting to another, review your medicines and how you take them, and help you with other chronic care needs.

For more information, ask your healthcare provider or visit the official Medicare website, where you can find global and local resources for chronic disease management.

Mental Health Support

To ensure you can get help and encourage reaching out during a crisis, Medicare covers a range of Mental health support services available through Medicare during a health crisis, emphasizing the importance of seeking help when needed. The scope of coverage may vary depending on the plan, with Medicare Advantage Plans including fewer items.

On the other hand, Medicare Part B covers counseling, specialized treatment, and many other outpatient mental health services, like substance abuse treatment. Medicare Part B may pay for a partial hospitalization for inpatient services, provided a licensed professional can certify you need this treatment. Your costs will be covered by Medicare Part A (hospital services) and Medicare Part B (services provided by a healthcare provider in the hospital if you need full hospitalization for mental health issues.

5.7. advocating for yourself: how to dispute charges and appeal decisions

Understanding Medicare Statements

You must know how to accurately read your Medicare statements to advocate for yourself successfully. It will help you identify potential errors or charges you don't agree with.

Here is a quick guide to reading Medicare statements:

1. Go over the claims to ensure your provider's name, procedure code, and service date match the services for which it's been issued.
2. Go to the front page and check if your deductibles (Part A and Part B, if you have the latter) have been met.
3. Check each claim to verify payments were made properly. While doing so, answer the following questions:

   a) Did Medicare pay toward each?
   b) Were the expenses, payments, and benefit days broken down correctly?
   c) If you had services for a skilled nursing facility or hospital, was the copay for these claims, correct?
   d) If it was a claim covered by Medicare Part B, was it paid 80% on Medicare's parts and 20% on yours?

Filing a Dispute

Step 1: Determining Where and How You Want to File Your Dispute

You can dispute charges or coverage decisions through The Centers for Medicare & Medicaid Services. They provide information in several accessible formats, including large print, braille, audio files, TTY communication, and relay services. The time limit for filing disputes varies among plans, but requesting an accessible service will not affect this (the time it takes to receive them is added to the time you must take action).

Step 2: Make Contact

You can request information regarding a dispute through:

- CMS Medicare Phone Number: 1-800-MEDICARE (1-800-633-4227)
- CMS Fax Number: 1-844-530-3676 3
- The following address: Centers for Medicare & Medicaid Services Offices of Hearings and Inquiries (OHI) 7500 Security Boulevard, Mail Stop S1-13-25 Baltimore, MD 21244-1850
- Your plan if you are enrolled in a Medicare drug or Medicare Advantage Plan

Step 3: Provide All the Necessary Details

Regardless of how you file your claim, you must provide your name, phone number, the information you need (if known), and the mailing address where they should send the received documentation.

Navigating the Appeals Process

If you disagree with the expenses determined by Medicare about your policy, coverage, costs, etc., you can file an appeal. For example, if you require medication or specialized services for your condition, you can use the appeals process to request coverage from Medicare. You can also ask Medicare to change your out-of-pocket expenses for drugs, services, or medical supplies.

Beneficiaries can appeal if their claims were denied because of an unrelated open accident record, their coverage for frequent abuse is denied, or their plan stops paying for services, medication, or supplies they still need.

Here is how to appeal:

1. Ask your health care or medical supply provider or pharmacists for documentation to support your claim. Consult your specific Medicare plan to see what information you must provide.
2. After gathering the necessary documentation, fill out a Redetermination Request Form and send it to the company handling Medicare claims for your plan. You'll find their contact information on your summary notice.
3. Alternatively, you can send a written request to the company with your name, address, and the Medicare number on your Medicare card, the list of items or services in question, dates of services, your

reasoning for requesting coverage, your Medicare representative name (if you have one), and other information that may help your case.

4. After you've submitted your appeal, you must wait for the decision on your claim. You'll receive it within the next 60 days.

5. If you disagree with the decision you receive, you can submit a second appeal. There are three levels of appeal, and at each, you'll receive written information on how to proceed if you want to move to a higher level.

Resources and Support

Resources and organizations that can aid and represent during the dispute and appeals processes are:

- Medicare: You can file an appeal through Medicare.gov/forms-help-resources/medicare-forms.
- State Health Insurance Assistance Program (SHIP)

5.8. the mental health coverage of medicare: what is included

Scope of Coverage

Medicare covers a wide range of mental health services, including:

- Yearly depression screening in a primary care doctor's office or a clinic that offers referrals to mental health specialists or follow-up treatment if necessary.
- The first preventive visit after enrolling in Medicare.
- Yearly mental health wellness visits for consulting a healthcare provider about potential changes in the patient's mental health during the past year.
- For those already receiving mental health therapy, additional testing is needed to verify whether they're getting the necessary help and if it's helping them.
- Psychotherapy (individual or group) with licensed mental health professionals.
- Additional treatment perks like family counseling (if necessary for the patient's healing).
- Complete psychiatric evaluation and additional diagnostic tests.
- Psychiatric medication management.
- Administration of prescription drugs that can only be given by medical professionals (for example, injections).
- Partial hospitalization for mental health issues.

Accessing Mental Health Services

Depending on whether you've bought Medicare Advantage or Original Medicare, you may access mental health services by finding a mental health professional or through a referral to your primary care physician. Those on the Original Medicare plan rarely need prior authorization but can benefit from a referral, making finding the right therapist easier.

By contrast, those on Medicare Advantage plans will likely need a referral or authorization from a primary care doctor in the Medicare network. Remember, these plans are often more specific with coverage and will have a narrower range of professionals within their network.

Contact your health plan to verify whether you need a referral and which providers and services you can use to avoid confusion and unnecessary expenses. If you don't need a referral, you can find a mental health professional through one of the tools enlisted in this book or the official Medicare website.

Medication and Therapy Coverage

Medicare offers coverage for psychiatric medications and therapy sessions by therapists licensed in the state where they offer the services. However, there might be limitations or copays in some cases. Each plan has specific approved amounts to cap the payout. Medicare Part B pays 80% and you pay the other 20%, as well as the coinsurance and deductible. The same applies to psychiatric evaluation.

If you get hospitalized for a psychiatric condition, Medicare Part A may cover all your inpatient costs, while Medicare Part B pays to cover the services provided by the medical personnel. Hospital costs in a psychiatric facility are covered for up to 190 days, after which a decision is made whether you can be transferred to a general hospital or remain in the psychiatric unit. If you're transferred,

Medicare Part A may take care of your general hospital costs.

Other forms of counseling may be covered by Medicare, like family sessions needed to advance treatment for psychological conditions and grief counseling and prevention. The coverage only applies if a state-licensed clinical psychologist or psychiatrist perform the services.

Medicare Part B covers the costs of a single depression evaluation a year. This can be done in a primary care facility and performed by a doctor who can refer patients for treatment or follow-up visits. New beneficiaries are entitled to a preventative consult, where their risks for depression are revised.

While Medicare D doesn't cover all psychiatric medications, most plans provide coverage for antipsychotics, antidepressants, and anticonvulsants.

Breaking the Stigma

Mental health is an underrated portion of people's health. People often feel judged for seeking help or criticized for not dealing with their mental health conditions.

Remember, mental health is as crucial for your well-being as physical health. Don't be afraid to seek help when needed. With the ever-widening range of services available through Medicare, access to support has never been easier. So, feel free to take advantage.

5.9. looking ahead: preparing for healthcare needs in late retirement

Anticipating Healthcare Needs

Discuss the importance of anticipating potential healthcare needs as beneficiaries age, including common health issues and how to plan for them.

Long-Term Care Options

Here are a few long-term care options to consider:

- **Home-and-Community-Based Services:** These allow you to remain connected to a supportive community and are suitable for those who don't need round-the-clock care. Usually, they are not covered by Medicare but may be covered by local organizations.
- **Subsidized Senior Housing:** A great option for low-income retirees. Usually, it is not covered by Medicare as it doesn't include medical care.
- **Continuing Care Retirement Communities (CCRCs):** Suitable for those requiring round-the-clock care due to chronic conditions. Some services may be covered by Medicare.
- **Hospice and Respite Care:** End-of-life services for most conditions are covered by Medicare, but it is best to consult your plan about these.

- **PACE (Program of All-inclusive Care for the Elderly):** As a Medicare program, PACE is covered by Medicare plans, including prescription drugs, nursing care, and other essential services.

For more information about long-term care and funding, talk to your social worker or discharge planner or reach out to organizations like the Center for Independent Living (CIL), Area Agency on Aging (AAA), and Aging and Disability Resource Center (ADRC). Native individuals can also talk to their local healthcare providers for information about funding their long-term care.

Advance Directives

Advance directives, including living wills and healthcare proxies, are tools to help ensure your wishes are respected when you can no longer communicate. This information should be included in everyone's medical records so that healthcare professionals, retiree organizations, loved ones, and attorneys know how to act when you become incapacitated. They enable friends and family to speak for you in situations you've designated or when you can't speak for yourself.

Advance directives may not be the easiest thing to do, but they can give everyone peace of mind if the worst happens. Making critical decisions about someone's life can be overwhelming. So, by outlining what interventions you want and don't want, you're removing a burden from your loved ones. It minimizes their stress and reduces the likelihood of potential conflicts.

An advance directive can help you as a beneficiary by enabling you to decide about avoiding unnecessary pain, unwanted hospitalization and expenses, useless procedures, and more.

Holistic Planning

Planning for retirement requires a holistic approach, meaning you must consider several factors that could influence your health and happiness during your later years. You can prevent and manage health conditions by caring for your physical health and mental well-being. However, to have a truly fulfilling retirement experience, you can't forget about financial planning and building strong social support. Medicare can be a great tool for covering your healthcare expenses, but ensuring you have the tools and support to stay healthy and recover will go a long way toward fulfilling your retirement dreams.

6
mastering medicare: insider tips and strategies

Understanding tips and strategies about Medicare can be advantageous. It enables you to maximize your coverage by comprehending the scope of services covered and navigating the system effectively. Ultimately, this knowledge enhances navigating the healthcare system, ensuring timely access to necessary care, better health outcomes, and financial security.

6.1. leveraging free medicare resources: counseling and support

Maximizing SHIP Resources

State Health Insurance Assistance Programs (SHIP) provide invaluable support for Medicare beneficiaries. These programs offer personalized counseling and assistance tailored to individual needs. SHIP counselors are trained to help you understand your Medicare coverage options, including Original Medicare, Medicare Advantage, and Medicare prescription drug plans (Part D). Counselors can help you compare plans based on cost, coverage, and provider networks, helping you make informed decisions.

SHIP counselors provide unbiased information and can help you navigate complex Medicare issues, like coverage gaps, appeals, and billing questions. These services are typically free or offered at low cost, making them accessible to all Medicare beneficiaries.

Utilizing Medicare.gov's Tools

Medicare's official website, Medicare.gov, offers a range of tools and resources to help you manage your Medicare coverage effectively.

The Plan Finder tool allows you to compare Medicare Advantage plans, Medicare Prescription Drug Plans (Part D), and Medicare Supplement Insurance (Medigap) policies based on your specific needs and location.

Medicare.gov provides access to publications, forms, and educational materials to help you stay informed about Medicare changes, enrollment periods, and important deadlines. The website is user-friendly and regularly updated to ensure accurate and current information.

Medicare Interactive Toolbox

The Medicare Rights Center offers an interactive toolbox called Medicare Interactive that provides comprehensive information and resources for navigating Medicare. The toolbox includes guides, fact sheets, and interactive tools to help you understand various aspects of Medicare, like eligibility, coverage options, and enrollment. Medicare Interactive is a trusted information source endorsed by organizations like the Centers for Medicare & Medicaid Services (CMS) and the Social Security Administration (SSA).

Community-Based Programs

Many local community organizations and agencies offer programs and resources to support Medicare beneficiaries. These programs include educational workshops, counseling services, support groups, and assistance in navigating Medicare-related issues. Community-based organizations often collaborate with SHIP programs and other agencies to provide comprehensive support and advocacy for Medicare beneficiaries. These programs are tailored to specific communities' needs and offer culturally sensitive services and language assistance.

6.2. insider tips for reducing out-of-pocket expenses

Annual Cost Reviews

Reviewing your out-of-pocket costs annually to ensure you have the most cost-effective Medicare plan for your needs is crucial. Examine your healthcare expenses from the past year, including premiums, deductibles, copayments, and coinsurance. Compare these costs to the available Medicare plans in your area, considering monthly premiums, annual deductibles, coverage limits, and out-of-pocket maximums.

Use Medicare's Plan Finder tool or consult a SHIP counselor to compare plans and identify changes or updates affecting your costs. Consider factors like changes in your health status, prescription drug needs, and anticipated healthcare expenses for the upcoming year.

Lowering Prescription Costs

Prescription medications can be a significant source of out-of-pocket expenses for Medicare beneficiaries. Still, there are several strategies for reducing these costs. Review your current medications and discuss cost-saving options with your healthcare provider or pharmacist. Consider using preferred pharmacies that offer discounted pricing on prescription drugs.

Explore mail-order pharmacy services that often provide convenient delivery options and discounts or lower copayments for 90-day medication supplies. Ask your healthcare provider about generic alternatives to brand-name medications, usually substantially cheaper and are typically covered by Medicare Part D plans.

Furthermore, inquire about prescription assistance programs offered by pharmaceutical companies or charitable organizations that provide financial assistance or discounts for eligible individuals.

Benefiting from Preventative Services

Medicare covers various preventative services at no cost, including screenings, vaccinations, and counseling services. Taking full advantage of these preventative services helps you avoid future health expenses by detecting potential health issues early or preventing them altogether.

Schedule regular wellness visits with your healthcare provider to discuss your preventive care needs and ensure you're up to date on recommended screenings and vaccinations. Standard Medicare-covered preventative services include annual wellness exams, mammograms, colorectal cancer screenings, flu shots, and smoking cessation counseling.

Medigap Enrollment Timing

Medigap policies, or Medicare Supplement Insurance, can help cover out-of-pocket costs not covered by Original Medicare. Carefully consider the timing of enrolling in a Medigap policy to ensure you get the best coverage options and rates.

The best time to enroll in a Medigap policy is during your open enrollment period, which begins when you're 65 or older and enrolled in Medicare Part B. During these six months, you have guaranteed issue rights, meaning insurance companies cannot deny you coverage or charge you higher premiums based on pre-existing conditions.

If you miss your open enrollment period, you may still enroll in a Medigap policy later. However, you could be subject to medical underwriting, which may result in higher premiums or coverage denials based on your health history.

Enrolling in a Medigap policy during the open enrollment period can secure lower premiums and ensure comprehensive coverage for out-of-pocket expenses associated with Medicare.

6.3. strategies for choosing the best medicare plan for your health needs

Assessing Personal Health Needs

Start by meticulously evaluating your current health status. Consider chronic conditions, ongoing medical treatments, or your regular healthcare needs. Reflect on recent doctor visits and medical procedures to gauge your healthcare requirements accurately.

Compile a comprehensive list of preferred healthcare providers, specialists, hospitals, and medical facilities. Note down the healthcare professionals you trust or have a long-standing relationship with.

Review your prescription medications, including dosages and frequency. Identify essential medicines you take regularly and ensure your insurance plan covers them.

Anticipate future healthcare needs by considering age-related health changes, potential medical procedures or surgeries, and family medical history. Consider whether you need additional healthcare services or treatments in the coming years.

Comparing Plan Features

Understand the distinct features and benefits of Medicare Advantage (Part C) plans and Medigap (Medicare Supplement Insurance) policies by delving into their nuances.

Medicare Advantage plans typically offer a bundled package of benefits, including coverage for hospital stays, doctor visits, and prescription drugs. Evaluate the benefits of different Medicare Advantage plans, like dental, vision, and hearing coverage, and assess whether they align with your healthcare needs.

Medigap policies work alongside Original Medicare (Parts A and B) to cover out-of-pocket costs like deductibles, copayments, and coinsurance. Explore the various Medigap plans available in your area and compare their coverage options, monthly premiums, and provider networks.

Scrutinize the fine print of each plan, paying attention to details like coverage limitations, network restrictions, and cost-sharing requirements. Consider how these factors impact your overall healthcare costs and access to care.

Considering Future Health Changes

Engage in forward-thinking by envisioning potential changes in your health status or healthcare needs over time. Consider factors like aging-related health changes, developing new medical conditions, or specialized medical treatments.

Evaluate the flexibility of each Medicare plan in adapting to future health changes. Assess whether the plan allows you to switch healthcare providers, access specialized care or medical facilities, or change your coverage during specific enrollment periods.

Anticipate life events that may impact your healthcare needs, like retirement, relocation, or changes in marital status. Ensure your Medicare plan can accommodate these life changes and provide continued coverage and support.

Utilizing Decision Support Tools

Leverage the power of online decision-support tools to streamline your Medicare plan selection process. Explore resources like Medicare.gov's Plan Finder tool, which compares Medicare Advantage and Part D plans based on your unique healthcare needs and preferences.

Take advantage of online calculators and comparison tools provided by insurance companies, healthcare organizations, and independent agencies. Input detailed information about your healthcare needs, prescription medications, budget, and preferences to receive personalized recommendations and cost estimates.

If you encounter challenges or uncertainties during decision-making, seek guidance from knowledgeable sources like SHIP counselors or healthcare professionals. Use their expertise to gain additional insights and perspective on choosing the best Medicare plan for your health needs.

6.4. the importance of reviewing your medicare plan annually

Understanding Open Enrollment

Medicare Open Enrollment, or the Annual Enrollment Period (AEP), occurs annually from October 15th to December 7th.

During this period, Medicare beneficiaries can change their coverage for the upcoming year. Open Enrollment can be your primary chance to review your current Medicare plan and adjust if necessary. This period allows you to switch between Original Medicare and Medicare Advantage, change Medicare Advantage plans, enroll or switch Part D prescription drug plans, or make other changes to your coverage.

Keeping Up with Plan Changes

Medicare plans can change their benefits, costs, provider networks, and coverage areas yearly.

Stay informed about annual changes to their Medicare plans by carefully reviewing the Annual Notice of Change (ANOC) or Evidence of Coverage (EOC) documents sent by the plan provider. Furthermore, pay close attention to changes in premiums, deductibles, copayments, coinsurance, and coverage limitations.

Remember, failing to review these changes could result in unexpected costs or coverage gaps impacting your access to necessary healthcare services.

Evaluating New Medicare Options

New Medicare Advantage and Part D plans are introduced each year, offering access to more coverage options and potentially enhancing your healthcare needs. Explore new Medicare plan options during the Open Enrollment period to see if plans provide improved benefits, lower costs, or expanded coverage.

Furthermore, never assume your current plan is the best option. Constantly evaluate all available choices to ensure you get the most value from your Medicare coverage.

Seeking Professional Advice

Seek professional advice during the Open Enrollment period to make informed decisions about Medicare coverage. Consulting with a Medicare expert, such as a licensed insurance agent specializing in Medicare or a State Health Insurance Assistance Program (SHIP) counselor, is advisable.

6.5. how to leverage medicare during hospital stays and home care

Navigating Hospital Coverage

Understanding Medicare coverage during hospital stays to avoid unexpected costs and ensure comprehensive care is crucial.

Medicare Part A typically covers inpatient hospital stays, including semi-private rooms, meals, general nursing, and other hospital services and supplies.

You must understand the distinction between inpatient and observation status. Inpatient status typically triggers Medicare Part A coverage. Observation status may result in higher out-of-pocket costs as it's considered outpatient care.

You should advocate for yourself by asking about their status, clarifying coverage details with hospital staff, and appealing if they believe you should be classified as an inpatient rather than an observation.

Maximizing Home Health Care Benefits

Medicare offers home health care benefits to eligible beneficiaries who require skilled nursing care, physical therapy, speech-language pathology services, or intermittent skilled nursing care at home.

To qualify for Medicare home health care benefits, you must meet specific criteria, including being homebound and requiring skilled care prescribed by a doctor.

Covered home health care services include wound care, medication management, medical equipment, and assistance with daily living activities.

It would be best to work closely with your healthcare providers and home health agencies to ensure you receive the appropriate care and maximized Medicare benefits for home health services.

Coordinating with Other Insurance

Many Medicare beneficiaries have additional insurance coverage, like employer-sponsored insurance or Medigap policies that supplement Medicare coverage during hospital stays.

Understanding how your other insurance coverage interacts with Medicare to avoid benefits duplication or coverage gaps is vital.

Communicate with healthcare providers, insurance companies, and Medicare to coordinate coverage effectively and ensure you receive the maximum benefits under the various insurance plans.

Post-Hospitalization Care

After a hospital stay, you may require additional care in skilled nursing facilities, rehabilitation centers, or through home health care services.

Medicare Part A covers skilled nursing facility care for eligible beneficiaries who meet specific criteria, including a prior hospital stay of at least three consecutive days.

Plan for post-hospitalization care by discussing discharge plans with your healthcare providers, understanding your Medicare coverage options for skilled nursing and rehabilitation services, and researching available facilities or home health agencies.

You must follow up with their healthcare providers and Medicare to ensure a smooth transition from hospital to post-hospital care and to address coverage or care coordination issues.

By leveraging Medicare coverage effectively during hospital stays and home care, you ensured receiving the necessary care and support, minimizing out-of-pocket costs and confidently navigating the healthcare system's complexities.

6.6. understanding medicare's coverage of alternative medicine

Exploring Covered Services

Medicare coverage of alternative medicine services is limited compared to conventional medical treatments. Still, certain services may be covered for specific conditions.

Chiropractic services are among the alternative treatments covered by Medicare. Medicare Part B typically covers chiropractic adjustments when medically necessary to correct subluxation of the spine.

Acupuncture is another alternative therapy Medicare covers for specific conditions. As of 2021, Medicare covers up to 12 acupuncture sessions over 90 days for chronic low back pain that lasts at least 12 weeks without responding to conventional treatments.

Other alternative medicine services, like massage therapy, naturopathy, or herbal medicine, are generally not covered by Medicare. However, you may explore supplemental insurance options or pay out of pocket for these services if desired.

Supplementing Medicare with Additional Insurance

While Medicare provides coverage for certain alternative medicine services, you can seek supplemental insurance to access broader coverage for alternative treatments.

Medigap (Medicare Supplement Insurance) plans offer additional coverage for alternative therapies not covered by Original Medicare, like acupuncture, chiropractic care, or other complementary and alternative medicine (CAM) treatments.

Medicare Advantage plans may cover alternative medicine services beyond what Original Medicare covers. However, you should carefully review the plan details to understand coverage limits, provider networks, and out-of-pocket costs for alternative treatments.

Advocating for Coverage

Beneficiaries who believe specific alternative medicine treatments may benefit their health should work with their healthcare providers to advocate for coverage under particular circumstances.

Discuss alternative treatment options with your healthcare provider and obtain their support and recommendation.

Document medical evidence supporting the efficacy of the alternative treatment for your condition, like research studies, clinical trials, or expert opinions.

Submit a formal request for coverage to Medicare, including supporting documentation and a letter of medical necessity from your healthcare provider outlining why the treatment is medically necessary for your condition.

Staying Informed about Expanding Coverage

Medicare coverage of alternative medicine services may evolve in response to ongoing research, clinical evidence, and policy changes.

Hence, stay informed about changes in Medicare coverage for alternative medicine by regularly reviewing updates from the Centers for Medicare & Medicaid Services (CMS) and other reputable sources.

Keep abreast of emerging research on the efficacy and safety of alternative treatments for various health conditions.

Advocate for broader coverage of alternative medicine by participating in advocacy efforts, contacting policymakers, and sharing your experiences with alternative treatments and their impact on your health and well-being.

6.7. niche strategies for couples, singles, and those with dependents

Customizing Strategies for Different Life Stages

Couples: Coordinating Medicare benefits can be advantageous for couples. They can explore joint enrollment in Medicare Advantage plans or Medigap policies to ensure comprehensive coverage for both partners. Considerations include comparing premiums, deductibles, and coverage options for the most cost-effective solution for both individuals.

Singles: Singles should optimize their Medicare coverage to meet their individual needs. They can choose plans based on their specific healthcare requirements, like selecting a Medicare Advantage plan with comprehensive coverage or a high-deductible Medigap plan to minimize monthly premiums.

Those with Dependents: Beneficiaries with dependents, like adult children or elderly parents, must consider the impact of their Medicare decisions on their dependents' healthcare needs. They should evaluate their coverage options to ensure adequate coverage for themselves and their dependents and consider household budgeting, caregiver responsibilities, and potential long-term care needs.

Couples Coordinating Benefits

Couples can maximize their Medicare benefits by coordinating their coverage and choosing complementary plans that meet both partners' healthcare needs.

Timing enrollment is critical for couples, especially if one partner is eligible for Medicare before the other. They must coordinate enrollment to avoid coverage gaps and ensure continuous healthcare coverage.

Couples should compare their Medicare options, including Original Medicare with Medigap coverage or Medicare Advantage plans, to determine the best combination of benefits, premiums, and out-of-pocket costs for their unique situation.

Considerations include evaluating whether joint or separate enrollment in Medicare plans offers the most cost-effective solution for both partners based on health status, prescription drug needs, and provider preferences.

Singles Maximizing Medicare Value

Singles should focus on maximizing the value of their Medicare coverage to meet their healthcare needs and minimize out-of-pocket costs.

They should opt for Medicare Advantage plans with comprehensive coverage and additional benefits, like prescription drug coverage, dental, vision, and hearing benefits.

Alternatively, singles could choose a high-deductible Medigap plan to keep monthly premiums low while providing coverage for catastrophic medical expenses.

Singles should carefully review plan details, including provider networks, drug formularies, and out-of-pocket costs, to ensure their Medicare plan meets their healthcare needs and budget.

Considering Dependents in Medicare Planning

Medicare beneficiaries with dependents must consider how their healthcare decisions impact their household budgeting and healthcare planning.

They should assess their coverage options to ensure adequate healthcare coverage for themselves and their dependents, considering age, health status, and anticipated healthcare needs.

Depending on the situation, you may need to explore options for long-term care coverage, like purchasing additional insurance or setting aside funds for future care needs.

You must communicate openly with your family members about their healthcare plans and involve them in decision-making processes to ensure everyone's needs are adequately addressed.

6.8. maximizing benefits: utilizing preventative services and wellness programs

Comprehensive Use of Preventative Services

Medicare offers various preventative services to maintain health and detect potential health issues early. These services include screenings, vaccinations, counseling, and annual wellness visits.

These services reinforce the importance of using available preventative services covered by Medicare to prevent or detect health conditions in their early stages, often more treatable and less costly to manage.

Please familiarize yourself with the covered preventative services available under Medicare Part B and schedule them according to your healthcare provider's recommendations and Medicare guidelines.

Staying up to date with preventative care helps you avoid more serious health issues, improve overall health outcomes, and reduce healthcare costs.

Engagement in Wellness Programs

Medicare offers various wellness programs to promote healthy behaviors and improve well-being. One notable program is SilverSneakers, which provides Medicare beneficiaries access to fitness facilities, exercise classes, and wellness resources.

Active participation in Medicare-covered wellness programs includes improved physical fitness, better management of chronic conditions, reduced risk of falls and injuries, and enhanced social connections.

Explore available wellness programs in your community or through your Medicare plan and actively participate in activities aligning with your interests and health goals.

Regular exercise and participation in wellness programs can contribute to better health outcomes and quality of life, ultimately leading to a more active and fulfilling lifestyle.

Tracking Preventative Service Use

Track your preventative services and wellness programs to ensure you take full advantage of their Medicare coverage. Maintain a personal health record or calendar to track when you receive preventative services, like screenings, vaccinations, and wellness visits.

Schedule regular check-ups with your healthcare provider to discuss your preventative care needs and ensure they are up to date with recommended screenings and vaccinations.

Educating on the Value of Prevention

Understand the long-term value of engaging in preventative care and wellness programs as a proactive approach to maintaining health and well-being. Investing time and effort in preventative care now can significantly save healthcare costs by preventing or managing chronic conditions, reducing costly medical treatments or hospitalizations, and improving overall quality of life.

Furthermore, take personal responsibility for your health by adopting healthy lifestyle behaviors, participating in preventative care, and actively engaging in wellness activities. Remember to view preventative care not only as a means of preventing illness but also as investing in your future health and longevity, ultimately leading to a more vibrant and fulfilling life.

6.9. future-proofing your medicare: anticipating changes and staying informed

Monitoring Medicare Policy Changes

Stay informed about legislative and policy changes impacting your Medicare benefits and coverage options, like changes to Medicare laws, regulations, reimbursement rates, and program updates. Regularly check official Medicare communication channels, like the Centers for Medicare & Medicaid Services (CMS) website, Medicare.gov, and the Medicare & You handbook, for updates on policy changes and program updates.

Subscribe to newsletters, follow Medicare-related news outlets, and join online communities or forums dedicated to Medicare to stay informed about the latest developments and discussions surrounding Medicare policy.

Flexible Planning for Future Healthcare Needs

Adopting a flexible approach to Medicare planning is crucial for accommodating changes in health needs. Regularly review your Medicare coverage options and consider how changes in your health status, lifestyle, or financial situation impact your healthcare needs.

Engaging in Medicare Advocacy

Active participation in advocacy efforts can shape future Medicare policies to benefit you and your fellow beneficiaries. Get involved in advocacy organizations dedicated to Medicare issues, like AARP, the Medicare Rights Center, or the National Committee to Preserve Social Security and Medicare.

Contact elected representatives, participate in grassroots campaigns, attend town hall meetings, and share personal stories to illustrate the necessity of Medicare benefits and advocate for policy changes supporting beneficiaries' needs.

Leveraging Technology for Medicare Management

Technology is increasingly significant in managing healthcare and Medicare benefits, offering tools and resources to help beneficiaries stay organized, informed, and connected.

Leverage technology for Medicare management, like using online portals and mobile apps provided by Medicare plans to access benefit information, review claims, and track healthcare expenses. Furthermore, explore telehealth services, electronic health records, and wearable health devices to monitor your health status, communicate with healthcare providers, and access virtual care options from the comfort of your home.

exploring medicare innovation and alternative models

Exploring Medicare Innovation

Medicare is continually evolving, with ongoing efforts to innovate and improve the delivery of healthcare services to beneficiaries. Therefore, exploring emerging innovations in Medicare, like value-based care models, accountable care organizations (ACOs), and telemedicine services, is a great way to stay informed. Value-based care models aim to improve healthcare quality and outcomes while reducing costs by incentivizing providers to deliver efficient and effective care.

Likewise, ACOs unite groups of healthcare providers who collaborate to coordinate care for Medicare beneficiaries, focusing on improving care coordination, reducing duplicative services, and enhancing patient outcomes.

Benefits of Exploring Medicare Innovation

Exploring Medicare innovation is an excellent way to access new care delivery models, technologies, and services that improve the healthcare experience and outcomes.

Value-based care models and ACOs prioritize preventive care, care coordination, and patient engagement, leading to better management of chronic conditions, reduced hospital admissions, and improved overall health outcomes.

conclusion

With a system as complex as Medicare, you need all the help you can get to obtain your healthcare (and possible retirement) goals. As you age, the risks of needing medical care and related services increase, and making informed decisions on covering related expenses is paramount for a fulfilling retirement experience.

Making decisions about paying for future healthcare needs can be overwhelming, particularly if you do not understand how you can receive assistance. Whether due to disability, lack of availability, language or cultural barriers, or other factors, many struggle to understand Medicare. Despite being one of the best tools for medical expense coverage, Medicare is surrounded by many misconceptions and misunderstandings. With a determined mission to demystify Medicare and provide peace of mind for those who consider enrolling, this book covered the crucial concepts of the

Medicare system, including its parts, functions, benefits, and more.

Breaking down the information into easy-to-understand bits is the core of making Medicare accessible and understandable for adults and seniors. By embarking on this remarkable journey, you've gained valuable insights into the complex issues causing many headaches to current and potential beneficiaries.

Besides the comprehensive information regarding the crucial concepts, you also received step-by-step instructions and guidance for the various stages of Medicare management. You've learned what it takes to enroll in the Medicare program and how to choose the best plan based on your current and possible future needs, budgets, and other requirements. You read about the possibilities of navigating healthcare after retirement, whether in the near future or if you plan to work for several more years after turning 65 and want to prepare for late retirement.

Making informed decisions is key in retirement planning. It applies to the financial and healthcare aspects. Understanding Medicare and your options and rights will affect both aspects because you can't plan for either without knowing what to expect from your insurance policy. With the guidance and resources you've received in this book, you can keep track of policy changes, healthcare needs, and other information you need to make empowered decisions.

The value of leveraging resources can't be stressed enough. Nowadays, people have a wealth of resources available, including SHIP, Medicare.gov, and various tools and apps, to assist in their Medicare journey. Moreover, these sources keep expanding as quickly as the list of services and providers under Medicare's umbrella.

Due to the deep interconnectedness of healthcare and financial planning, looking beyond what Medicare can offer is advisable. For example, enrolling in Medicare when they become eligible at 65 may be a good option for some individuals. But it may not fit someone else's needs (especially if they work and have comprehensive health insurance through their employer).

For the same reason, you should consider the bigger picture and focus on long-term planning instead of Medicare enrollment and which plan to choose. You can better decide about your retirement plans by evaluating your future needs and calculating possible expenses. Proper financial planning can make a vast difference in barely being able to afford anything and genuinely enjoying your retirement years.

Ensuring you get the best care through and with Medicare assistance takes a team effort. However, much of it comes down to you. As you have the right to receive the proper care without financial strain, you also have an obligation to remain engaged and advocate for yourself in healthcare settings. By actively engaging with your healthcare providers and building a trust-filled relationship, participating in Medicare policy discussions, and standing up for your rights and needs within the Medicare system, you're cementing the foundations for a better, more secure future.

If you don't understand something related to your care or plan, ask your doctor or plan provider. Be honest and ask as many questions as necessary. It's always better to ask more than to regret not asking enough later.

The Medicare system is incredibly fluid, so you'll need ongoing education to stay on top of Medicare and related healthcare matters. Moreover, your healthcare needs can change with age, and you'll likely need to adapt your coverage and planning to your changing needs. It is natural, and consequently, it shouldn't be disregarded. Otherwise, you may incur unexpected costs and loss of valuable time.

Investing in your health through proper care, preventive measures, and long-term healthcare planning is one of the best investments you can make in your life. Like any investment, Medicare requires proper considerations and regular check-ups (health and financial) to ensure you get the optimal returns.

Receive my sincere gratitude for embarking on this Medicare planning journey, affirming my commitment to helping others navigate their healthcare futures confidently. Assisting in navigating the Medicare maze is an incredibly rewarding experience, and hopefully, by finding empowerment to meet your healthcare needs, you'll find it as fulfilling.

Please share your opinion about your journey throughout the book by leaving a review. May it serve as a steppingstone for your future learning and assist in educating others who require help with Medicare. Besides the helpful information you learn from these, please share your experiences and questions with plan and healthcare providers, fostering a community of support and shared learning around Medicare planning.

Likewise, by talking about your experience with elements of Medicare, you are more likely to encounter people who are or have been in the same boat as you and can offer their valuable insight. It is another step toward establishing a supportive community. Don't let yourself or anyone else suffer the consequences of misinformation and have their health affected by a lack of knowledge about getting financial assistance for diverse medical needs. You have the power to make a change, even if it's small. If everyone else in your community does at least the same, little by little, the small changes will add up. This is how many changes in the Medicare system have been made in the past and how many more can be made in the future.

references

"Medicare Summary Notice" (MSN) | Medicare. (n.d.). Www.medicare.gov. https://www.medicare.gov/basics/forms-publications-mailings/mailings/costs-and-coverage/medicare-summary-notice

2023 Medicare Parts A & B Premiums and Deductibles 2023 Medicare Part D Income-Related Monthly Adjustment Amounts | CMS. (2022, September 27). Www.cms.gov. https://www.cms.gov/newsroom/fact-sheets/2023-medicare-parts-b-premiums-and-deductibles-2023-medicare-part-d-income-related-monthly

5 Ways to Get Help with Prescription Costs |Medicare.gov. (n.d.). Www.medicare.gov. https://www.medicare.gov/drug-coverage-part-d/costs-for-medicare-drug-coverage/costs-in-the-coverage-gap/5-ways-to-get-help-with-prescription-costs

Barrett, A. (2024, February 7). How Can Medicare Deliver for Changing Health Needs Over the Next 40 Years? (Part two). Croakey Health Media. https://www.croakey.org/how-to-ensure-medicare-delivers-for-changing-health-needs-over-the-next-40-years-part-two/

Bunis, D. (2023, December 14). Big Medicare Changes in 2024. AARP; AARP. https://www.aarp.org/health/medicare-insurance/info-2023/future-medicare-changes.html

CDC. (2022, October 31). Getting Health Care During Travel | Travelers' Health | CDC. Wwwnc.cdc.gov. https://wwwnc.cdc.gov/travel/page/health-care-during-travel

Centers for Medicare & Medicaid Services. (n.d.). Centers for Medicare & Medicaid Services Data. Data.cms.gov. https://data.cms.gov/tools

CMS. (2020, March 17). Medicare Telemedicine Health Care Provider Fact Sheet. Www.cms.gov. https://www.cms.gov/newsroom/fact-sheets/medicare-telemedicine-health-care-provider-fact-sheet

Compare Medigap Plan Benefits | Medicare. (n.d.). Www.medicare.gov. https://www.medicare.gov/health-drug-plans/medigap/basics/compare-plan-benefits

Comprehensive Wellness Centers. (n.d.). Medicare Coverage of Mental Health Services. Medicare & Medicare Advantage Info, Help and Enrollment. https://www.medicare.org/articles/medicare-coverage-of-mental-health-services/

Costello, A. (2023, October 16). Planning Your Federal Retirement: FEHB vs Medicare. FEDweek. https://www.fedweek.com/retirement-benefits/planning-your-federal-retirement-fehb-vs-medicare/

Cottrill, A., & 2023. (2023, September 18). What to Know about the Medicare Open Enrollment Period and Medicare Coverage Options. KFF. https://www.kff.org/medicare/issue-brief/what-to-know-about-the-medicare-open-enrollment-period-and-medicare-coverage-options/

Drug Assistance Programs | AAFA.org. (n.d.). Asthma & Allergy Foundation of America. https://aafa.org/advocacy/advocacy-resources/patient-assistance-medicine-drug-programs/

Get Help with Costs | Medicare. (n.d.). Www.medicare.gov. https://www.medicare.gov/basics/costs/help

GoHealth. (n.d.-a). Does Medicare Cover Pre-existing Conditions? GoHealth. https://www.gohealth.com/medicare/coverages-benefits/pre-existing-conditions/#medigap-and-pre-existing-conditions

GoHealth. (n.d.-b). What Does Medicare Part C Cover? | Advantage Coverage. GoHealth. https://www.gohealth.com/medicare/medicare-advantage/coverage/

Hall, A. (2023, November 2). Medicare Advantage Is Complicated—Here's How Older Adults Can Navigate Open Enrollment Successfully. Forbes Health. https://www.forbes.com/health/medicare/changes-in-medicare-advantage/

Home. (n.d.). State Health Insurance Assistance Programs. https://www.shiphelp.org/

How to Apply For Medicare: A Complete Step-by-Step Guide. (n.d.). RetireGuide. https://www.retireguide.com/guides/how-to-sign-up-for-medicare/

In Neighbor. (2024, February 21). What is a SHIP in Medicare, and How Does it Benefit Me? Insurance Neighbor. https://www.insuranceneighbor.com/what-is-ship-in-medicare-how-does-it-benefit-me

Items and services excluded from Medicare coverage - Medicare Interactive. (2018). Medicare Interactive. https://www.medicareinteractive.org/get-answers/medicare-covered-services/medicare-coverage-overview/items-and-services-excluded-from-medicare-coverage

Krupa, A. (2021, September 23). Medicare Advantage vs. Medicare Supplement (Medigap): Which Is Best? Forbes Health. https://www.forbes.com/health/medicare/medicare-advantage-vs-medicare-supplement/

Lamboley, L. (2020, March 2). 5 Recommendations for the AWV Personal-ized Prevention Plan. Blog.prevounce.com. https://blog.prevounce.com/5-recommendations-for-awv-personalized-prevention-plan

Lankford, K. (2023, March). When Do I Sign Up for Medicare If I'm Working at Age 65? AARP; AARP. https://www.aarp.org/health/medicare-qa-tool/do-i-enroll-in-medicare-age-65-even-if-still-working.html

Lee, J. (2021, August 17). How to Choose a Medigap Policy. GoodRx; GoodRx. https://www.goodrx.com/insurance/medicare/how-to-choose-a-medicare-supplement-plan#choosing-a-medigap-plan

Medicare Education | Direction Home Akron Canton. (n.d.). Www.dhad.org. https://www.dhad.org/resources-education/medicare-education

Medicare Interactive. (2015, September 3). Steven Did not Sign up for Medicare When He was First Eligible. Medicare Interactive. https://www.medicareinteractive.org/resources/case-studies/mr-b-did-not-sign-up-for-medicare-when-he-was-first-eligible

Medicare Interactive. (n.d.-a). Health Savings Accounts (HSAs) and Medicare. Medicare Interactive. https://www.medicareinteractive.org/get-answers/coordinating-medicare-with-other-types-of-insurance/job-based-insurance-and-medicare/health-savings-accounts-hsas-and-medicare

Medicare Interactive. (n.d.-a). Medicare Coverage for Those who live Perma-nently Outside the United States. Medicare Interactive. https://www.medicareinteractive.org/get-answers/medicare-health-coverage-options/medicare-and-living-abroad/medicare-coverage-for-those-who-live-permanently-outside-the-united-states

Medicare Interactive. (n.d.-b). Making Part B enrollment decisions with VA benefits. Medicare Interactive. https://www.medicareinteractive.org/get-answers/coordinating-medicare-with-other-types-of-insurance/veterans-affairs-va-benefits-and-medicare/making-part-b-enrollment-decisions-with-va-benefits

Medicare Interactive. (n.d.-b). Tips to find a Medicare doctor. Medicare Interactive. https://www.medicareinteractive.org/get-answers/planning-for-medicare-and-securing-quality-care/getting-quality-care/tips-for-finding-a-doctor

Medicare Interactive. (n.d.-c). Medicare Coverage of Telehealth Services. Medicare Interactive. https://www.medicareinteractive.org/get-answers/medicare-covered-services/medicare-coverage-overview/medicare-coverage-of-telehealth-services

Medicare Interactive. (n.d.-d). Traveling with Medicare. Medicare Interactive. https://www.medicareinteractive.org/get-answers/medicare-covered-services/medicare-coverage-overview/traveling-with-medicare

Medicare Made Clear. (n.d.-a). Medicare Coverage for Non-Working Spouses. Www.uhc.com. https://www.uhc.com/news-articles/medicare-articles/medicare-coverage-for-non-working-spouses

Medicare Made Clear. (n.d.-b). Why You and Your Spouse Might Need Different Medicare Plans. Www.uhc.com. https://www.uhc.com/news-articles/medicare-articles/why-you-and-your-spouse-might-need-differ ent-medicare-plans

Medicare Plan Finder Gets an Upgrade for the First Time in a Decade | CMS. (2019, August 27). Www.cms.gov. https://www.cms.gov/newsroom/press-releases/medicare-plan-finder-gets-upgrade-first-time-decade

Medicare. (2019). What Are My Other Long-Term Care Choices? | Medicare. Medicare.gov. https://www.medicare.gov/what-medicare-covers/what-part-a-covers/what-are-my-other-long-term-care-choices

Medicare. (n.d.-a). Avoid Late Enrollment Penalties | Medicare. Www.medicare.gov. https://www.medicare.gov/basics/costs/medicare-costs/avoid-penalties

Medicare. (n.d.-a). Chronic Care Management Coverage. Www.medicare.gov. https://www.medicare.gov/coverage/chronic-care-management-services

Medicare. (n.d.-b). Emergency Room Services Coverage. Www.medicare.gov. https://www.medicare.gov/coverage/emergency-department-services

Medicare. (n.d.-b). Medicare Coverage Outside the United States. https://www.medicare.gov/Pubs/pdf/11037-Medicare-Coverage-Outside-United-States.pdf

Medicare. (n.d.-c). How Do I File an Appeal? | Medicare. Www.medicare.gov. https://www.medicare.gov/claims-appeals/how-do-i-file-an-appeal

Medicare. (n.d.-c). When Does Medicare Coverage Start? Www.medicare.gov. https://www.medicare.gov/basics/get-started-with-medicare/sign-up/when-does-medicare-coverage-start

Medicare. (n.d.-d). Urgently Needed Care Coverage. Www.medicare.gov. https://www.medicare.gov/coverage/urgently-needed-care

Medicine, F. (2015, August 10). Patient-Doctor Relationship: Good or Bad? Scripps Health. https://www.scripps.org/news_items/5394-8-ways-to-build-a-strong-relationship-with-your-doctor

National Association of Insurance Commissioners. (2023, October 26). Three Ways to Protect Yourself During Medicare and Medicare Advantage Open Enrollment. NAIC. https://content.naic.org/article/three-ways-protect-yourself-during-medicare-and-medicare-advantage-open-enrollment

National Conference of State Legislatures. (2022, October 26). State Pharmaceutical Assistance Programs. Www.ncsl.org. https://www.ncsl.org/health/state-pharmaceutical-assistance-programs

NewPrimaryCare.com. (2022, June 24). How to Switch Doctors & Medicare Primary Care Physicians. New Primary Care. https://www.newprimarycare.com/learning-center/npc-doctor-complement-medicare-plan/

Original Medicare vs. Medicare Advantage: Which Should I Choose? | Medicare. (n.d.). Www.humana.com. https://www.humana.com/medicare/medicare-resources/original-medicare-vs-medicare-advantage

Pan Foundation. (n.d.). Everything You Need to Know About Medicare Reforms. PAN Foundation. https://www.panfoundation.org/everything-you-need-to-know-about-medicare-reforms/

Petkevich, D. (2023, April 19). Why Is Medicare So Confusing? Fair Square Medicare. https://fairsquaremedicare.com/articles/medicare-confusion

Ready to sign up for Part A & Part B | Medicare. (n.d.). Www.medicare.gov. https://www.medicare.gov/basics/get-started-with-medicare/sign-up/ready-to-sign-up-for-part-a-part-b Boyles, M. (2023, May 15). 7 key benefits of EHR systems. Northeastern University Graduate Programs. https://graduate.northeastern.edu/resources/benefits-of-ehr-systems/

Rosenberg, A. (2024, February 15). What Is Medigap? What to Know About Medicare Supplement Plans. NerdWallet. https://www.nerdwallet.com/article/insurance/medicare/medigap-what-to-know-about-medicare-supplement-insurance

The National Council on Aging. (n.d.). Www.ncoa.org.https://www.ncoa.org/article/understanding-medicare-s-late-enrollment-penalties

UCI Health. (n.d.). Benefits of Advance Directives | UCI Health | Orange County, CA. Www.ucihealth.org. https://www.ucihealth.org/patients-visitors/advance-care-planning/benefits-of-advance-directives

Vision Retirement. (2023, August 7). How to Transition from Private Health Insurance to Medicare. Vision Retirement. https://www.visionretirement.com/articles/transitioningtomedicare

webadmin. (2022, March 30). How and Why to Read a Medicare Summary Notice (MSN). Wisconsin Senior Medicare Patrol. https://www.smpwi.org/how-and-why-to-read-a-medicare-summary-notice-msn/

Williams, B., Dulio, A., Claypool, H., Perry, M., & Cooper, B. (2004). Waiting for Medicare: Experiences of Uninsured People With Disabilities in the

Two-Year Waiting Period for Medicare. https://www.commonwealth fund.org/sites/default/files/documents/

Wiseradvisor Insights. (2019, August 16). 5 Steps for Incorporating Healthcare in Retirement Planning - WiserAdvisor - Blog. Wiseradvisor. https://www.wiseradvisor.com/blog/retirement-planning/incorporating-health care-in-retirement-planning/